An Omega Institute Mind, Body, Spirit Book

Contemplative Living

❖

Joan Duncan Oliver

A DELL TRADE PAPERBACK

A DELL TRADE PAPERBACK

Published by
Dell Publishing
a division of
Random House, Inc.
1540 Broadway
New York, New York 10036

Series consulting editor: Robert Welsch
Series editor: Kathleen Jayes
Series Manager: James Kullander
Literary Representative: Ling Lucas, Nine Muses and Apollo, Inc.

Library of Congress Cataloging in Publication Data

Oliver, Joan Duncan.
    Contemplative living / Joan Duncan Oliver.
        p.   cm. — (The Omega Institute mind, body, spirit series)
    Includes bibliographical references and index.
    ISBN 0-440-50869-X (pbk.)
    1. Meditation.   2. Self-actualization (Psychology)—Religious
aspects.   I. Title.   II. Series
BL627.043   2000
291.4′4—dc21   99-39248
                                                          CIP

Printed in the United States of America
Published simultaneously in Canada
January 2000

10 9 8 7 6 5 4 3 2 1

RRD

BOOK DESIGN BY JENNIFER ANN DADDIO

Your future is determined by who you have chosen to honor! (Listen for the sound of honor)

ABOUT OMEGA

Omega was founded in 1977 at a time when holistic health, psychological inquiry, world music and art, meditation, and new forms of spiritual practice were just budding in American culture. Omega was then just a small band of seekers searching for new answers to perennial questions about human health and happiness. The mission was as simple as it was large: to look everywhere for the most effective strategies and inspiring traditions that might help people bring more meaning and vitality into their lives.

Since then, Omega has become the nation's largest holistic learning center. Every year more than 25,000 people attend workshops, retreats, and conferences in health, psychology, the arts, and spirituality on its eighty-acre campus in the countryside of Rhinebeck, New York, and at other sites around the country. While Omega has grown in size, its mission remains the same. Omega is not aligned with any particular healing method or spiritual tradition. Its programs feature all of the world's wisdom traditions and are committed to offering people an opportunity to explore their own path to better health, personal growth, and inner peace.

The name Omega was inspired by the writings of Teilhard de Chardin, a twentieth-century mystic and philosopher who used the word to describe the point within each one of us where our inner spiritual nature meets our outer worldly nature. Teilhard believed that the synthesis of these two domains presented the greatest challenge—and the greatest hope—for human evolution. Of his belief in the balance between world and spirit, Teilhard wrote, "I am going to broadcast the seed and let the wind carry it where it will."

Omega has taken on the task of helping spread that seed so that a better world for all of us can continue to take root and grow.

OMEGA
Institute for Holistic Studies

Mandy
616-340-0136

The Omega Institute
Mind, Body, Spirit Series

The Essentials of Yoga

Vitality and Wellness

Writing Your Authentic Self

Bodywork Basics

Contemplative Living

The Power of Ritual

Omega Institute sends out heartfelt thanks and appreciation
to staff members and teachers for their support
and contribution in the preparation
and publishing of this book.

Contents

One

❖

Starting

Out

What Is Contemplative Living?

The mystery of life is and always has been
the central focus of the contemplative mind.

—RABBI DAVID A. COOPER

Life is complicated and the rate of change astounding. We see the evidence all around us. Computers allow us to calculate and communicate at speeds beyond imagining. The Internet is spreading like the mile-a-minute vine, so that we're all connected at the click of a mouse. Everything that happens at any time, anywhere, is accessible to almost everyone on the planet. But behind the sprawling technological edifice we now inhabit, many people sense that there must be, in the words of one best-seller, *Something More.*

Bookstores are filled with antidotes to life in the fast lane, many of them with *simple* in the title: *The Simple Living Guide, Simple Abundance, Plain and Simple, Living the Simple Life,* to name a few. Even the business magazines that regularly offer advice on getting "the competitive edge" are now also touting ways to achieve a balanced life. How ironic that at a time of unprecedented prosperity many of us are longing for less. And in a world of unparalleled opportunity, we're wondering how to cut back on our activities and reduce stress.

More than a century ago Henry Thoreau observed that "our life is frittered away by detail" and admonished, "Simplicity, simplicity, simplicity." We're finally taking his advice to heart. Today, more and more of us are looking for ways to slow down, step back from the daily hubbub, and find the underlying meaning of our lives. In a recent survey by *Fast Company*, a cutting-edge business magazine, over 90 percent of the respondents said the number one priority for achieving balance was "making personal life more of a priority." For some of us achieving balance may be a kind of distant hope—something to get to when our schedule clears. For others the task is urgent. As Pir Vilayat Inayat Khan, head of the Sufi Order of the West, warns in *Awakening*, "It is important to ask yourself how you will feel if you continue living in the same way until the age of eighty—for by ignoring the needs of your soul, you run the grave risk of dying in despair."

It may seem as if you can't get off the fast track without depriving your family or endangering your career. And, like most people, you may legitimately have overlapping demands on your time and energy. But the irony is that the more you push yourself, the more you threaten the happiness and well-being you're after.

That's where the notion of contemplative living comes in.

Contemplative Living

What does it mean to lead a contemplative life? Fifty years ago the answer was simpler. A contemplative life was a cloistered life, in the shelter of a monastery or convent or hermitage or forest. It was a life devoted to spiritual practice, to meditation and prayer.

Today, a contemplative life—a thoughtful or meditative life—doesn't require running off to a mountaintop or joining a religious order. We may make a brief retreat now and then, for rest and renewal, but never has the call been louder to remain in the world, going about our business. For most of us, contemplative living means finding joy and serenity in the midst of everyday existence and expressing that equanimity in our relations with others. "Harmonious and balanced living is not only the preparation for contemplation but also the practice of contemplation and its ultimate goal," the late Les Hixon tells us in *Coming Home*, his overview of enlightenment in the world's mystical traditions.

In one sense contemplative living means being conscious. A definition of *consciousness* is "freedom from attachment." Your identity is no longer tied up in your car or your house or your job—or even in your talents or innovative ideas. On a broader level being conscious can be characterized in three words: *Awake. Alive. Aware.* There's a vibrancy to people who are truly, deeply conscious. We sense that they know something important, that they've "done the work"—the psychological and spiritual work of understanding themselves and recognizing their part in something larger.

We all fall somewhere along the spectrum from "sound asleep" to "enlightened," and at any given moment our behavior announces to the world how awake we are. In a now-famous lecture at the Menninger Foundation, Ram Dass, one of America's best-loved spiritual teachers, said:

> The only thing you have to offer to another human being, ever, is your own state of being … *everything you do, whether you're cooking food or doing therapy or being a student or being a lover,* you are only doing your own being, you're only manifesting how evolved a consciousness you are. *That's what you're doing with another human being. That's the only dance there is!*

How to reach and maintain a state of open awareness in the dance of life is what this book will explore.

Beginning the Quest

Every quest begins with a question. If you're reading this sentence, it's likely you've already begun to reexamine your priorities. Perhaps you're wondering how to get off the treadmill and find more time for yourself and your family. Perhaps your concerns are psychological—how to deal with anxiety, or depression, or fear. Maybe your issues are situational: Why does your life feel out of control? What can you do to change it?

One of our biggest challenges today, as management consultant James Ballard points out in *What's the Rush?*, is to regain a sense of inner control amid the vagaries of modern living. "Even though we don't have much control over events and circumstances," he notes, "we can train ourselves to be assured of an internal control that brings us peace and well-being."

For most of us the first reaction to a speeded-up world is to run faster in an effort to keep up. That may work for a while, but inevitably, like a clock that's wound too tight, our springs give out and the mechanism breaks down. Change today is happening too quickly and in too many places at once for us to adjust and recover in the ways we've relied on in the past.

What is required, as everyone from time-management experts to Tibetan Buddhist lamas are now suggesting, is a complete reconsideration of the way we approach life. Our most important tool isn't a faster modem or a smaller cell phone or a bigger bank account but a more expansive and reflective state of mind. That will allow us to draw on our most valuable inner resources—intuition and empathy—to approach life's challenges creatively, with compassion for ourselves and others.

Psychologist Daniel Goleman, author of the best-seller *Emotional Intelligence*, points out that the word *contemplation* comes from the Latin *com* (with) and *templum* (temple); it originally meant the attention given to laying out the ground for a temple. "Contemplation sacralizes the ordinary, divining its deepest dimensions," he states in a paper prepared for The Project on the Contemplative Mind in Society. "In its deepest sense it connotes an awareness directed toward a sacred end."

What begins as our desire for a calmer, saner existence often leads us into deeper territory—spiritual exploration. In *Journey of Awakening*, his classic work on meditation, Ram Dass explains:

> *The game of awakening is very subtle. At first you may buy the package of meditation because you're nervous, anxious, uptight. You want to get rid of all your pain and have a little pleasure out of life. But you really don't know what you're buying. They say, meditate and you can have a Cadillac, but they don't tell you that . . . [b]y the time you get to the Cadillac who it was that*

wanted it isn't around anymore. See the predicament? Meditation changes your desires in the course of fulfilling them.

What we want, in the end, is enlightenment, though we may not realize that at the outset of the journey.

Modern Mystics

Americans are among the most religious people on earth—96 percent of us say we believe in God or a universal spirit, 90 percent of us pray, and more than two thirds belong to a church or synagogue. But 70 percent of us think it's possible to be religious without attending services, according to a Gallup poll. Significantly, the fastest-growing religion in America is Buddhism. Much of the attraction is due to Buddhism's emphasis on meditation and contemplative practice. A survey by Wade Clark Roof, J. F. Rowney Professor of Religion and Society at the University of California, Santa Barbara, found that a majority of baby boomers prefer meditating alone to worshipping at communal services. The growing popularity of meditation is one indicator of the upsurge in desire for a direct, personal experience of God or the divine or whatever name you give to the sacred source.

The Path of Healing

Before we search for God, however, we usually look for more immediate satisfaction. Meditation and prayer are widely recognized as effective stress-management methods. They can help us handle life at warp speed with poise and equanimity. Instead of trying to avoid problems through compulsive activity, we can use prayer and meditation to help us find solutions within ourselves.

Contemplative practices enable us to handle fear and anxiety in creative ways.

Rather than trying to eliminate negative emotions—an impossible task—we can choose to explore them. When a disturbing feeling arises, we can take the time to observe it closely, to uncover its exact nature. In that way we come to see that, good or bad, everything passes. With the support of meditation and prayer, we learn to make friends with change and to view our own areas of vulnerability as opportunities for emotional and spiritual growth.

In many indigenous societies the spiritual leader is the shaman, the "wounded healer." Through healing his own pain he gains the power to transmute the suffering of others. Like the shaman we can become the agents of our own healing, drawing strength from a contemplative practice to deal with death, divorce, ill health, and life's other setbacks and losses. Father Thomas Keating, a Benedictine monk and author, calls the spiritual journey "a form of divine psychotherapy in which God tries to heal us on every level."

The Path of Wisdom

Meditation and prayer are more than just effective tools for healing, however. They are age-old technologies of spiritual transformation, found in one form or another in every faith tradition.

Spiritual practice may already be part of your life. In that case your question might be: How can I deepen my spiritual connection? Or: How can I find a practice that's closer to my heart? This book explores dozens of different ways to respond to those inner promptings—practices that focus the mind, center the body, and bring us to union with the divine. "God is in the details," it has been said. In a holographic universe each tiny molecule mirrors the pattern of the whole. From that perspective every small gesture of goodwill, of understanding, of simple attention to others, is a form of contemplative practice—a means of connecting with the awareness that each of us is a manifestation of the One.

"It wouldn't take much for us to be fully present, and then to give that gift of attention—which is like a gift of love—to others," suggests Sharon Salzberg, an American Buddhist teacher who is cofounder of the Insight Meditation Center in Barre,

Massachusetts. A regular spiritual practice can take us to a deeper level of contemplative living—a place of inner wisdom. It allows us to recover something profound we may not even know has been missing. As poet and naturalist Diane Ackerman explains in *Deep Play:*

> *People have lost spirituality from their lives, a sense of belonging to the pervasive mystery of nature, of being finite in the face of the infinite, of minimizing themselves and feeling surrounded by powerful and unseen forces. They've also lost a concern with such higher values as compassion, altruism, forgiveness, and mercy. Dispensing with God does not have to mean dispensing with a sense of the sacred and its attendant values. It's natural for humans to crave spirituality.*

Heeding the Call

Increasingly, scientists are looking in the structures and chemistry of the brain for physical evidence that we're spiritual beings. There's even talk of a "spiritual gene"—something in our DNA that makes us thirst for meaning. Religious literature is full of stories about ordinary folk who've had sudden, life-transforming conversions. Even if you are not yet ready to commit to a spiritual practice, you can at least begin to open your mind to the mystery that lies at the core of our being.

"Few people actually receive big calls, such as visions of flaming chariots and burning bushes," author and workshop leader Gregg Levoy points out in *Callings.* "Most of the calls we receive and ignore are the proverbial still, small voices that the biblical prophets heard, the daily calls to pay attention to our intuitions, to be authentic, to live by our own codes of honor."

Let's be very clear: the contemplative life is not a goody-goody life, pious and hypocritical and unreal. Even the highest teachers imaginable, those of great spiritual attainment, are human and therefore have shortcomings. Most of us will be working on our shadows—disowned feelings and capabilities relegated to the unconscious—throughout our lives. Contemplative life does not demand—or promise—perfection. What spiritual practice gives us is the means to weather the storm. We will constantly be thrown off balance by reality—by shifts in our emotional winds, disappointments, and ego blows. Prayer and meditation are rafts that can ferry us across rough water to safe harbor.

"Our practice is all we have," points out author and counselor Heide Banks. "Whether our practice is meditation or service or studying with a spiritual teacher, practice keeps us remembering what's important."

The Way Home

Coming home is a universal metaphor for self-realization, or enlightenment—the feeling of oneness or union with the divine that is the fruit of the spiritual journey. Settling into a spiritual practice that suits you often feels like a "mini" homecoming. There is an intuitive rightness about it, as if your whole being—body, mind, heart, and soul—is in tune.

That's not to suggest that the spiritual path is a straight way to heaven. It's more like the Yellow Brick Road. There are bound to be detours and doubts and hazards—not to mention times when the fog is so thick, you despair of even seeing your goal. Throughout this book there are suggestions for how to deal with resistance and to pick yourself up and begin again. The great life lesson of meditation, wise teachers say, is that it teaches us how to start over.

There is a famous twelfth century Zen teaching, commonly known as the Ten Ox-Herding Pictures, that describes the steps toward enlightenment or realizing your true nature—what in Zen is called Original Mind. The ox represents our true nature, the heart of the spiritual quest.

In the first picture the man is searching for the ox. Here we are, awakening to our spiritual longing. But the text asks the question: Why are we searching, when nothing has been lost? We are, in fact, never separate from our own true nature; the problem is, we don't realize that at first.

In the next picture the man spies the ox's footprints—gets a glimpse of the truth. He still lacks deep awareness, but at least he knows what direction to head in. Now he understands that truth isn't something "out there" but within himself. In the third picture the man spots the ox; he sees that to realize the truth, he must let go of his conditioned thinking and self-assumptions. In the fourth picture the man catches the ox, but it lurches about wildly; it's all he can do to hang on. This teaches us that although we may momentarily grasp the essential unity underlying the apparent duality of the world, our old habits of thinking are hard to break. We still need to develop self-discipline and honest self-examination, and to clear up unresolved issues from the past.

The fifth picture shows the man taming the ox. He can now hold fast to his practice and maintain moment-to-moment awareness. In the sixth picture, the stage of enlightenment, the man mounts the ox and rides it home whistling, his worries apparently over.

But this is only the apparent end of the journey. In the seventh picture the ox has vanished; this is called "Ox Forgotten, Self Alone," or "Ox Transcended." At this stage, we understand the power of the mind and the necessity to maintain right thinking. The eighth picture is an empty circle—both man and ox have disappeared. At this advanced stage of mind training, we stop identifying with the idea of a separate self. Reality just *is*. The ninth frame shows the reemergence of form; we see that the everyday world is merely the infinite taking on different shapes. In the tenth and final frame the fully enlightened one reenters the marketplace—everyday life—radiating compassion and kindness in his dealings with others.

Thus, the circle of transformation is completed. First, we perceive the world through dualistic eyes, seeing ourselves as unique individuals, distinct from one another. Then, with continued meditation practice, we may have a momentary experience of unity, when the distinction between self and other drops away, and we feel our oneness with all being. Finally, with the "wisdom eye" opened, we can grasp the paradox of being at the same time individuals and inseparable from the whole. This wider perspective allows us to participate fully in life, accepting all its joys and sorrows.

Living with Soul

A contemplative life is lived from our depths. It calls us to engage in every moment and every aspect of our existence. In *Care of the Soul* Thomas Moore, a former psychotherapist and Catholic priest, popularized the idea that happiness depends on reintroducing soul into our intimate lives. In *The Re-Enchantment of Everyday Life* he goes a step farther, suggesting that the widespread disaffection in the world today is the result of being cut off from our spiritual core. The antidote, he suggests, is to infuse daily life with a sense of wonder and maintain "a positive love of life amid many kinds of torment."

That means we must not ignore problems or injustices or pain—our own or others'. Instead, we can learn what Zen masters have long taught: that when we sit down in the midst of a problem, there is no longer a separation between us and the problem—so there's no problem. Fully facing and embracing the truth dissolves conflicts.

The Spiritual Renaissance

Today we are in the midst of a spiritual renaissance, as more and more of us strive to connect with the truth at our inner core. Many of us are searching for spirituality that fits us as individuals, rather than trying to squeeze ourselves into the precut styles of traditional religion. In this "postdenominational era," as it's often called, choices abound. It seems unlikely we'll return to the old religious affiliations—at least in the conventional ways. "Not since the cataclysm of World War II have most of us been able simply to adopt the meanings and values handed down by our parents' religion, our ethnic heritage, our nationality," Wade Clark Roof states in *A Generation of Seekers*, his study of baby boomer spiritual journeys. "Rather, what really matters became a question of personal choice and experience."

This is not to say that the faith of our fathers (and mothers) will be tossed out altogether. Although many churches and synagogues are closing their doors, others are rebuilding their congregations through reinvention and "renewal" movements. New or long-forgotten practices—some from other faiths—are being integrated into traditional services to create forms of worship that are relevant to the aspirations of seekers today. The height of such syncretism is the Techno Cosmic Mass, launched by the Catholic-turned-Episcopal priest Matthew Fox, father of Creation Spirituality. A multimedia, multicultural, interdenominational extravaganza inspired by England's all-night raves, it represents the ultimate in communal celebration of the Great Mystery, the longing for the divine.

Whether you prefer to sit silently in meditation, clap your hands and shout in exaltation, or do something in between, there is a path and a practice for you in the contemporary spiritual scene. We don't cover every alternative in this book, but we give you a sampling to suggest the scope of possibilities, and offer plenty of resources to help you set forth on your own.

Chapter 2, "Getting Ready," contains tools, including a self-quiz, to discover what form of practice might best suit you. Chapter 3, "Going Within," introduces the ideas of silence and solitude—keys to building a contemplative life. Chapter 4, "Finding Stillness," sets out the basics of meditation, including how to arrange time and space for spiritual practice. Chapter 5, "Mindfulness," introduces you to the concept underlying all contemplative practices—and to specific exercises to build conscious awareness into your life. Chapter 6, "Heart-Centering," contains instructions on practices that awaken caring and compassion. Chapter 7, "Meditative Prayer," teaches a variety of methods that go beyond the simple prayers of childhood. Chapter 8, "Celebrating Your Devotion," shows how to bring the senses into spiritual practice, through chanting, music-making, and sacred art. Chapter 9, "Moving with Spirit," suggests ways to involve the body in contemplative life. Chapter 10, "Staying on the Path," contains advice on overcoming doubt and resistance. Chapter 11, "Creating Community," discusses the benefits of being with other spiritual seekers. Chapter 12, "Into Action," reveals the fruit of contemplative practice—finding inner peace that brings joy to ourselves and others.

Building a contemplative life is a process. It won't happen overnight. It involves getting to know ourselves, dismantling our assumptions, letting go of our attachments, and ultimately, dropping our narrow, self-centered ways of looking at the world in favor of a broader spiritual perspective. In the end the mystical is, as the Zen masters say, Nothing Special. It is everyday life, approached as consciously as possible. As the late Abraham Maslow wrote in *Religions, Values, and Peak-Experiences*, "The great lesson from the true mystics, from the Zen monks, and now also from the Humanistic and Transpersonal psychologists, [is] that the sacred is in the ordinary, that it is to be found in one's daily life, in one's neighbors, friends, and family, in one's backyard...."

Let the journey begin.

RESOURCES

BOOKS

Ackerman, Diane. *Deep Play.* New York: Random House, 1999.

Ballard, James. *What's the Rush?* New York: Broadway, 1998.

Das, Lama Surya. *Awakening to the Sacred.* New York: Broadway, 1999.

Dass, Ram. *The Journey of Awakening.* New York: Bantam, 1978.

———. *The Only Dance There Is.* New York: Anchor Books, 1974.

Flickstein, Matthew. *Journey to the Center.* Somerville, Mass.: Wisdom Publications, 1998.

Goleman, Daniel. "The Contemplative Mind: Reinventing the News," a paper prepared for The Project on the Contemplative Mind in Society, 1996.

Hixon, Les. *Coming Home.* New York: Jeremy P. Tarcher, 1989.

Keating, Thomas. *Intimacy with God.* New York: Crossroad, 1996.

Khan, Hazrat Inayat. *The Inner Life.* Boston: Shambhala, 1997.

Khan, Pir Vilayat Inayat. *Awakening: A Sufi Experience.* New York: Jeremy P. Tarcher/Putnam, 1999.

Levoy, Gregg. *Callings.* New York, Harmony, 1997.

Maslow, Abraham H. *Religions, Values, and Peak-Experiences.* New York: Penguin, 1964.

Merton, Thomas. *New Seeds of Contemplation.* New York: New Directions, 1961.

———. *What Is Contemplation?* Springfield, Ill.: Templegate, 1981.

Moore, Thomas. *Care of the Soul.* New York: HarperCollins, 1992.

———. *The Re-Enchantment of Everyday Life.* New York: HarperCollins, 1996.

Reps, Paul. *Zen Flesh, Zen Bones.* Boston: Tuttle, 1998.

PERIODICALS

Common Boundary
7005 Florida Street
Chevy Chase, MD 20815
(301) 652–9495
bimonthly; spirituality, psychology, creativity

New Age
42 Pleasant Street
Watertown, MA 04172
(617) 926–0200
bimonthly; holistic living

Parabola
656 Broadway, Suite 615
New York, NY 10012
(212) 505–6200
quarterly; spirituality, myth, tradition

Spirituality & Health
74 Trinity Place
New York, NY 10006
(212) 602–0705
quarterly; soul in daily life

Utne Reader
1624 Harmon Place
Minneapolis, MN 55403
(612) 338–5040
bimonthly; alternative culture

What Is Enlightenment?
PO Box 2360
Lenox, MA 01240
(800) 376–3210
quarterly; spirituality

Yoga Journal
2054 University Avenue, Suite 302
Berkeley, CA 94704
(510) 841–9200
bimonthly; spirituality, health

WEB SITE

www.contemplativemind.org
Site of The Center for the Contemplative Mind in Society, which develops programs,
retreats, gatherings, and materials on integrating contemplative awareness into
contemporary life.

2.

Getting Ready

One truth, many doors.
—SWAMI SATCHIDANANDA

It is one thing to set out on a spiritual search but another to find the right practice. There's a familiar saying: When the pupil is ready, the teacher appears. Sometimes that's exactly what happens: you seem to be guided to just the right teacher—or teaching—at just the right moment. Perhaps a friend takes you to a talk that inspires you, or you wander into a yoga class while vacationing at a spa. Maybe a book "leaps off" a shelf into your arms as you're browsing in a local shop, or your sister tells you how much her life has changed since she started meditating.

Sometimes, though, the possibilities can seem overwhelming. What if, instead of one teacher or teaching, you discover too many? Or you're not sure what criteria to use in evaluating a path or practice—should you consider preference, convenience, what you hope to gain? Is a teacher necessary or advisable, or can you learn a method on your own? These are all legitimate questions that everyone considers in building a spiritual life.

Ancient Paths for Modern Seekers

In fact, finding the right path is an age-old issue. Even the ancients never assumed that in spiritual matters, one size fits all. Hinduism contains a number of different schools of yoga, some with roots going back thousands of years. Peter Tufts Richardson, a Unitarian Universalist minister who leads workshops on spiritual choice, based the four types of spiritual expression in his book *Four Spiritualities* on the yogas described in the *Bhagavad-Gita* (the Song of God), a 2,500-year-old epic poem often called the "gospel" of Hinduism. In this text Lord Krishna—an embodiment of the divine—instructs the warrior Arjuna in the path of knowledge (*jnana* yoga), the path of devotion (*bhakti* yoga), the path of right action (*karma* yoga), and the path of meditation (*raja* yoga).

In the centuries since, other forms of yoga have also become popular, including *hatha* yoga (cultivating the body), *mantra* yoga (using sacred sound), and *tantra* or *kundalini* yoga (the union of masculine and feminine energies). Each school embodies a different set of practices to move the seeker toward spiritual awakening. (*Yoga* literally means "yoke"; thus, yoga is the path by which one is "yoked to"—achieves union with—the divine.)

The different yogas recognize that talents and temperament incline each of us toward certain spiritual paths and away from others. Ramakrishna, the nineteenth-century Indian sage, noted that a good mother spices the same fish differently for each of her children, according to their taste—hot, mild, or subtle. So it is with spiritual practice.

Are you, for example, an intellectual sort, with a lively curiosity, a penchant for debate, and an ongoing love of learning? Then you are likely to be drawn to the path of knowledge and study—meditating on sacred texts or sacred images, for example.

Are you more physical, preferring sports or exercise to sitting around reading a book? Then movement practices such as hatha yoga, martial arts, or ecstatic dancing, or everyday activities such as walking and gardening would probably suit you best.

Are you introspective, an acute observer of yourself and human nature? You would probably find mindfulness practices such as Insight meditation and zazen powerful practices for self-discovery and spiritual attunement.

Are you creative, expressing your dreams and yearnings in poetry, music, journal-writing, or art? The path of creativity is an exhilarating one: think of Zen and Sufi poetry, Taoist painters, and medieval architects and artisans. The musically attuned could consider chanting, toning, or sound meditations.

Are you sensitive, moved to tears by a beautiful sunset or the plight of others, or touched to the core by the words of a spiritual teacher? A devotional practice such as chanting sacred names might suit you—or a heart-centered practice such as tonglen or lovingkindness meditation.

Are you a compassionate activist, committed to resolving the social, political, and environmental issues of our day, or even just to bearing witness to human struggle? This is the path of karma yoga—good works—embodied by people such as the Dalai Lama, Mother Teresa, and members of the Zen Peacemaker Order founded by Bernard Glassman Roshi. If you are drawn to this path you may or may not adopt a formal practice of meditation or prayer, but in either case you are likely to dedicate your life to service—even if that simply means becoming the most conscious real-estate broker in your office or the most attentive sales clerk in the store.

Your Spiritual Heritage

Previous religious training and experience also influence choices about a spiritual path. What is your religious background? Did you receive religious instruction? Was your family observant? Were you? Have you continued a religious practice into adulthood or let it lapse? How do you feel about your religious training now? Do you believe in God or a higher power? Would you call yourself agnostic?

We do not have to throw out the past to build a spiritual life for the present. "You may already own a whole chestful of spiritual tools that fit your hands exactly," suggests the American-born Tibetan Buddhist teacher Lama Surya Das in *Awakening to the Sacred* (see "Spiritual Tools," below). For example, you may have resented the strict training of Catholic school, but perhaps you loved the mystery of the mass—the incense and candlelight and intoning of the priests. Through a chanting practice or formal Zen training, for example, you could reconnect with your appreciation for ritual. Perhaps you have only a vague feeling of nostalgia for something you once felt but have forgotten: the desire to recover that sense of wonder could help you define your search.

For seekers today, there is a climate of inclusiveness. Putting together a contemplative life Chinese-menu style is acceptable in all but the most conservative religious circles. And many people, even spiritual teachers and the clergy, are finding that the practices of one tradition can deepen their faith in another. At a Zen or Insight meditation retreat it is not uncommon to discover that the person who's been sitting next to you all week is a monk or a nun, a rabbi or a minister.

At one Zen center where the week-long *sesshins*—retreats—customarily end at midday on Sunday, one regular participant was conspicuous for always leaving early, on Saturday afternoon. It turned out that he was a Presbyterian minister who faced a

Inspiration: Spiritual Tools

As you try to create your spiritual life from scratch, think about the spare parts and tools that you already possess. . . . Are there prayers that you already know by heart? Are there hymns and songs that speak to you as strongly now as they did when you were a child? Do you want to fast and pray for Yom Kippur? Do you want to go to church and be part of Good Friday and Easter? Don't hide from these impulses. No matter what your religious history, love is love; atonement is atonement; prayer is prayer; spiritual renewal is spiritual renewal.

—LAMA SURYA DAS, *AWAKENING TO THE SACRED*

long drive home to be on time for preaching the sermon at his church on Sunday morning. Another retreat participant at the same center was a Catholic nun, who had been practicing zazen for more than twenty years. Two or three times a year she left her cloister for retreat at the Zen monastery, crediting Zazen with deepening her connection to God and Jesus.

Sylvia Boorstein, a psychotherapist and meditation teacher who is a cofounder of Spirit Rock, an Insight meditation center in Woodacre, California, is one of a number of Americans raised as Jews who have gravitated to Buddhism. After a decade of Buddhist meditation practice she had a powerful experience that renewed her interest in Judaism. As she explains in *That's Funny, You Don't Look Buddhist*,

> *In the middle of a Buddhist meditation retreat my mind filled with a peace I had not known before—completely restful, balanced, alert, joyous peace—and I said, "Baruch Hashem" (Praise God). The next thing I did was say the Hebrew blessing of thanksgiving for having lived long enough, for having been "sustained in life and allowed to reach" that day. The blessings arose spontaneously in my mind. I didn't plan them. My prayer life in those days was a memory rather than a habit, but the blessing felt entirely natural.*

Buddhist meditation made her a more, rather than less, observant Jew, Boorstein says. These days she spends much of her time teaching Insight meditation to other Jews. Calling herself a "faithful Jew and a passionate Buddhist," she says, "I am grateful that I know two vocabularies of response. I think of one as my voice of understanding and the other as the voice of my heart."

Making Space for the Spirit

Practical matters also influence choices about contemplative practice. What is your current life situation? Are you working full-time? Do you have extensive family commitments? Is finding time or space for any spiritual activity a challenge? Or do you have the freedom and inclination to spend days, weeks, even months, concentrating on your spiritual life?

Whatever your circumstances or leanings there are practices to fit. A number of possibilities are set out in subsequent chapters. To help you begin the selection process, see the self-quiz ("Find a Practice") on page 22.

Some would argue that you can't find a spiritual practice by taking a quiz. "People should discover their own way," one meditation teacher, a psychotherapist, admonished. "The spiritual journey is so individual."

Indeed it is. No one would dispute that. And like any form of quiz or typology, the one in this book should be viewed only as a guide to self-discovery, not as a definitive statement of who you are. Preferences, personalities, even our deepest yearnings, can change—often dramatically—with time and experience. In today's post-denominational, multicultural world, we're developing our own definitions of spirituality and how to lead a contemplative life, mixing practices from different traditions in inventive ways, in an effort to find the meaning that we sense is buried somewhere beneath the busyness of our days.

Conventional wisdom says you should choose the practice that is most compatible; you're more likely to stick with it when you hit the inevitable moments of doubt and resistance. But the best practice is not necessarily the most comfortable, at least at first. Sometimes an inner prompting leads us to a practice that, on the surface, goes completely against type. Only much later do we recognize its significance in our spiritual advancement.

The issue comes down to what speaks to your divine yearning, to the questions or desires impelling you on a spiritual journey. This sense of individual responsibility is an essential element of what Elizabeth Lesser, one of Omega Institute's founders, calls the "cultural cross-breeding" of spirituality in America. "Many paths lead to spiritual freedom and peace," she writes in *The New American Spirituality.* "You are your own best authority.... You listen within for your own definition of spirituality. Your deeper longings are your compass on the search."

Try This: Find a Practice

Each of us has a natural way of relating to spirit—in some cases, more than one. And part of the adventure of the spiritual search is to find your own path home. But just as no one would require you to head into the wilderness without a map, there is nothing to prevent you from drawing on the experience of seekers who've gone this way before you.

The following exercise won't guarantee you a practice made in heaven. But it will lead you to some practices that people with similar personalities and interests have been drawn to in the past.

1. If you had a free afternoon, how would you most like to spend it? (pick two)

    a) Go for a long walk or run.

    b) Soak in the Jacuzzi or have a massage.

    c) See a romantic movie with your partner or friend.

    d) Enjoy a spectacular natural vista or the botanical gardens in bloom.

    e) Unplug the phone and curl up with a good book.

    f) Attend a lecture or language class.

    g) Volunteer at a literacy program or homeless shelter.

    h) Tidy up your home office.

2. Check all statements that apply:

    a) My family and friends are more important to me than anything else.

    b) I enjoy reading or writing poetry.

    c) I like singing or listening to music.

    d) I'm passionate about many things.

    e) I find discussion and debate stimulating.

    f) I like to understand the "why" and "how" of events.

g) I'm fascinated by what makes people tick.

h) I consider myself to be very observant.

i) When I read about human rights abuses or natural disasters, I try to find ways to help.

j) I am—or have been—politically active.

k) I consider work a spiritual practice.

l) I have donated time or money to a community or environmental cause in the past year.

m) I'm very concerned with diet and fitness.

n) I run, walk, or play a sport almost every day.

o) I don't like to sit still for too long.

p) I love to go dancing.

How to Score: Enter your responses on the form below. The category with the most checks is the one in which you will probably find a practice consistent with your lifestyle and values. If your score is the same in more than one category, consider trying practices from each.

THE WAY OF THE MIND

   1. e)

      f)

   2. e)

      f)

      g)

      h)

Practices: Mindfulness meditation, Insight meditation, zazen, psychospiritual work, inspirational reading, journal writing, contemplative prayer, shamanic journeying

THE WAY OF THE HEART

1. c)

   d)

2. a)

   b)

   c)

   d)

Practices: Prayer, *metta* (lovingkindness) meditation, *tonglen* (giving and receiving), *kirtan* (devotional chanting), contemplating sacred images, mantra meditation

THE WAY OF THE BODY

1. a)

   b)

2. m)

   n)

   o)

   p)

Practices: Yoga, t'ai chi, chi kung, aikido, walking, running, tracing the labyrinth, pilgrimage, trance dancing, painting, Sufi whirling, drumming

THE WAY OF ACTION AND SERVICE

1. g)

   h)

2. i)

   j)

   k)

   l)

Practices: Volunteer work, compassionate activism, mindful living, socially responsible investing, protecting the environment, gardening

Many Choices

Today's spiritual marketplace offers as many tantalizing choices as a well-stocked gourmet store. The Pluralism Project at Harvard University, developed by religion professor Diana L. Eck to study religious diversity in America, has identified fifteen major faith traditions practiced in the country today. Among these are hundreds of different sects with their own beliefs and practices. Faced with so many possibilities, how can you determine which one holds the key for you?

Spiritual counselors of every persuasion confront this question often. Some have devised categories to help seekers narrow their options. If, for example, you know which of the sixteen psychological types on the Myers-Briggs Type Indicator describes you, you can consult *Soul Types* by Sandra Krebs Hirsh and Jane A.G. Kise for suggestions on finding your "natural spiritual climate," as the authors put it. The MBTI, devised by Isabel Briggs Myers and her mother, Katherine C. Briggs, is based on the work of Carl Jung, who held that our innate, preferred ways of relating to ourselves and the world fall into certain categories.

We are either *Extroverted* (E) or *Introverted* (I), depending on whether we draw energy from our environment or from the inner world of ideas. (Do you, for example, feel more stimulated by being with a group of people or by having a heart-to-heart with one or two close friends?) We are *Sensing* (S) or *Intuitive* (N), depending on whether we are more likely to rely on information gathered directly through our five senses, or through insight, inference, and hunches. We are considered *Thinking* (T) or *Feeling* (F) types, depending on whether we base decisions primarily on objective criteria or on relational considerations, such as how those decisions might affect others. We are considered *Judging* (J) or *Perceiving* (P), depending on whether we tend to be decisive and seek closure, or to have an open-ended, let's-see-what-happens approach to life.

By these definitions, according to Hirsh and Kise, an introverted intuitive (INFJ or INTJ) would probably prefer solitary prayer and meditation, and a set time and place for spiritual practice, while an extroverted intuitive (ENFP or ENFJ) would gravitate to communal worship and a less structured spiritual life. Pragmatic sensing types—a majority of Americans—are generally attracted to more traditional modes of worship and to spiritual practices with concrete application to daily life, such as meditation for stress management.

Peter Tufts Richardson also draws on Jung's typology and the MBTI in *Four Spiritualities.* His four different "expressions of spirit" correspond not only to four classic schools of yoga but also to the four categories of personality outlined in the MBTI. Thus, intuitive types (NT), according to Richardson, are generally drawn to what he calls "the journey of unity"—practices in pursuit of truth, clarity of mind, and social justice. This path is analogous to jnana yoga—the cultivation of knowledge, or "divine awareness." The goal of jnana yoga, Richardson says, "is to hear about, mull over in the mind, sort, and ultimately realize the bliss of identification in Unity" through meditation. He cites the Buddha (the name means "the awakened one") and the twentieth century visionary Buckminster Fuller as "mentors" for seekers on this path.

Sensing-Feeling personalities (SF), exemplified by Muhammad and St. Francis of Assisi, are likely to gravitate to the "journey of devotion"—bhakti yoga—Richardson says. This path embodies what the mythologist Joseph Campbell once described as "the rapture of being alive." For seekers on this path "God is not a far-off, impersonal principle but rather a personal and approachable entity," Richardson says. Fitting practices include pilgrimage and service, as well as direct expressions of love for the divine in its many manifestations, through chanting, hymn singing, or other rituals.

Sensing-Thinking personalities (ST), according to Richardson, are most likely to follow a path of action—karma yoga, or doing good in the world. Those who walk this path tend to be life's realists—responsible, steadfast, and committed to doing what's right. Among the exemplars of this view is the seventeenth century Carmelite monk Brother Lawrence, who viewed his daily labors in the monastery kitchen as "the practice of the presence of God." As mentors for this path Richards suggests the Chinese sage Confucius, known for his practical advice, and the great Indian leader Mahatma Gandhi, who said, "Work is worship."

The Feeling-Intuitive type (FN) leans toward the "journey of harmony" in Richardson's model. This is the way of raja yoga—the quest for self-actualization, combined with deep feeling for others. To Richardson, Jesus and the early twentieth century Indian poet Rabindranath Tagore typify this journey. This is the way of the idealist, forever seeking deep knowing and the healing of self and others. "For those on this pathway," Richardson tells us, " 'Heal thyself' is always the starting place for spiritual growth."

Perceptual Style

Another way of uncovering the spiritual practices that would work best for you is to consider your perceptual style. Many meditation methods call for the ability to visualize—to create images with your inner eye. Skill in visualization varies widely. Although a majority of Americans are comfortable with the technique, some people find it nearly impossible. Their dominant perceptual mode is either auditory (hearing) or kinesthetic (a "felt-sense" in the body). People who are auditory dominant would probably enjoy sound-based meditations, such as chanting or drumming. Kinesthetic types would be likely to resonate with moving meditations, such as ecstatic dancing, martial arts, or walking the labyrinth.

To find out which perceptual type you are, you can use a tool from neurolinguistic programming (NLP), a method devised by John Grinder and Richard Bandler for understanding communication. Visual types tend to express their experience in visual imagery ("I see what you mean"), while auditory types use the language of sound ("I really hear you"), and kinesthetic types, sensory images ("I feel your pain"; "I grasp your meaning").

Seven Directions

Other systems can also help us identify our spiritual nature and find practices that speak to that yearning. Jami Sams, an artist of Cherokee and Seneca heritage, uses the seven directions (east, west, north, south, above, below, and within) of the Native American medicine wheel as a basis for the seven paths to enlightenment she sets out in *Dancing the Dream.*

> *Metaphorically, we are given seven paths to fully discover all parts of this beautifully diverse Creation and our human places within the whole. Because people respond to spirituality in different ways depending upon their Sacred Points of View, each spiritual tradition has different ways of marking the seven stages of growth and discovery, which are the human rights of passage. . . . Transformation is a personal journey that is directed by an individual's desire to explore the various paths.*

In *The Ways of the Mystic* Joan Borysenko, a Harvard-trained bioscientist, psychotherapist, and mystic, also draws on the medicine wheel in outlining seven paths to divine union. She links each path to one of the seven chakras (energy centers) that are central to yoga and incorporates elements of Buddhist, Christian, and Jewish Kabbalistic teachings and practice. "All religions lead to God, just the way all rivers empty into the sea," Borysenko points out. "God doesn't mind if you come by land or sea, on foot or by train, through the appreciation of beauty or the dedication of your life to others" (see "Paths to God," page 29).

How to Choose

These teachings are just a few of the ways to discover your spiritual direction. No matter how true your spiritual compass, choosing the right path takes time and thought. Just as you probably wouldn't agree to a major operation without a second or even third opinion, there is no harm in trying out several approaches until you find one that resonates with your personality, inner rhythm, values, and goals.

One woman who was anxious to develop a spiritual life spent more than a year sampling various traditions before she settled on Zen practice. In that time she attended meditation classes and talks at a local Tibetan Buddhist community, and at a center run by the Jains, an Indian sect that emphasizes strict asceticism and *ahimsa*—nonharm to all beings. She tried devotional yoga, chanting at the Siddha Yoga Foundation with followers of Swami Muktananda, and took up hatha yoga—a practice she still uses to stay supple and centered. She read spiritual books and kept a journal, attended services at two New Thought churches, Unity and Religious Science, and returned to the Episcopal Church, which she had not attended since early childhood. Then, one day, a friend pointed her toward a Zen center. She went inside for meditation instruction, and everything about the experience resonated, from the simple Japanese décor of the meditation hall to the woody smell of the temple incense to the discipline of zazen. "I realized I didn't want all the words and colors and activity of those other practices," she recalls. "At that time in my life I needed to develop a clean, clear view, because I was in such inner turmoil." In the years since, she has added Sufi whirling, *kirtan* (Hindu chanting), energy healing, hatha yoga, and psychospiritual study to her practice. But zazen remains the foundation on which her contemplative life rests. "The bottom line is, it grounds me," she says.

Inspiration: Finding a Path with Heart

When we ask, "Am I following a path with heart?" we discover that no one can define for us exactly what our path should be. Instead, we must allow the mystery and beauty of this question to resonate within our being. Then somewhere within us an answer will come and understanding will arise. If we are still and listen deeply, even for a moment, we will know if we are following a path with heart.

—JACK KORNFIELD, *A PATH WITH HEART*

Once you have found a practice that feels right, it is recommended that you stick with it long enough to experience some of its effects. A rule of thumb is to give a practice at least a few weeks; better still, a few months. Commit to it, agree to do the necessary disciplines, agree not to give up when it seems boring or hard. Then, if it feels wrong, move on to another practice. If you have a tendency to run when the going gets tough—bailing out of relationships or hometowns or jobs—you might want to think twice before you move on too quickly. On the other hand, there is no need to stick with a practice or philosophy that is clearly at odds with your temperament or values.

Whatever method you choose, it must ultimately satisfy only one criterion, the American Buddhist teacher Jack Kornfield, a cofounder of Spirit Rock Meditation Center, suggests in *A Path with Heart:*

In undertaking a spiritual life what matters is simple: We must make certain that our path is connected with our heart. *Many other visions are offered to us in the modern spiritual marketplace. Great spiritual traditions offer stories of enlightenment, bliss, knowledge, divine ecstasy, and the highest possibilities of the human spirit. . . . While the promise of attaining such states can come true . . . [t]hey are not the goal of spiritual life.*

The beloved teacher Ram Dass, in his classic work *Journey of Awakening*, offers a simple formula for picking a path: "Look at your life and see what has really turned you on." (See "Which Method Is for Me?," below.)

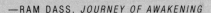

Inspiration: Which Method Is for Me?

People sometimes are turned off by meditation when they begin with a method that is too hard for them. It helps to use a method which uses your natural tendencies, and so reinforces a positive attitude. At the outset choose a method that harmonizes with what you are already good at, a method that interests you. Follow it until you feel a strengthened connection to a quietness of mind, to a meditative awareness, to God.

—RAM DASS, *JOURNEY OF AWAKENING*

That is not to say you won't move on to other practices eventually, as Ram Dass points out. The goal of contemplative living is to develop the whole person—body, mind, and heart, as well as the soul. Once you've mastered one form—say, Insight meditation—you may decide to take up a devotional practice to awaken your emotions, then add—or switch to—a moving practice, such as Aikido or trance dancing, to integrate your body into your spiritual life. If you're athletic or body-oriented, you might reverse the order.

The goal, in any case, is unity—within ourselves, and with the divine force. Time-tested vehicles for achieving that goal are the many forms of meditation, contemplation, and prayer.

Practice, Practice, Practice

Building a spiritual life isn't something you can do just by thinking about it. That would be like assuming you can lose ten pounds and tone your body without exercising. Meditation, contemplation, and prayer are exercises for the soul. Like physical workouts, they vary in form and difficulty, but all require some degree of attention and self-discipline. Even if your immediate goal is only to relieve stress and bring a little sanity into your life, you will need to be steadfast in your practice for it to be effective. There is a payoff to such persistence: Not only will you begin to know what clear thinking and peace of mind feel like but you are likely to get in touch with inner depths you may not have been aware of (see "Spiritual Transformation," below).

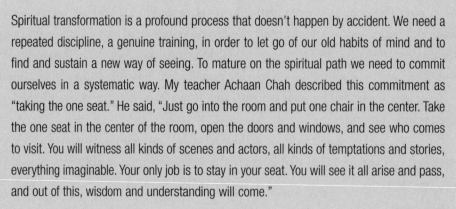

Inspiration: Spiritual Transformation

Spiritual transformation is a profound process that doesn't happen by accident. We need a repeated discipline, a genuine training, in order to let go of our old habits of mind and to find and sustain a new way of seeing. To mature on the spiritual path we need to commit ourselves in a systematic way. My teacher Achaan Chah described this commitment as "taking the one seat." He said, "Just go into the room and put one chair in the center. Take the one seat in the center of the room, open the doors and windows, and see who comes to visit. You will witness all kinds of scenes and actors, all kinds of temptations and stories, everything imaginable. Your only job is to stay in your seat. You will see it all arise and pass, and out of this, wisdom and understanding will come."

—JACK KORNFIELD, *A PATH WITH HEART*

What Is Meditation?

Meditation is a way to quiet the mind, increase our awareness, and develop self-understanding. *Sitting* is often used as a synonym for meditation; many forms of meditation are done by sitting still and erect on a cushion or chair. But there are also many types of moving meditation, such as walking, martial arts, and ecstatic dance.

Many forms of meditation are concentration practices—requiring you to focus on a word, an object, your thoughts, or your breathing. Others are practices of letting go, of releasing into a kind of hyperaware state in which you drop the endless chatter of your discursive mind and simply "go with the flow." Although there is a specific practice called "mindfulness," all forms of meditation are in a sense mindfulness meditations, in that they allow us to explore the workings of our minds and to reach an awareness of what the Buddhists call Mind—the essential unity underlying all.

Meditation can be done alone, or in a group. Studies show that it is not merely spiritual practice; it has beneficial effects for healing and stress management. Its great practical virtue is that you can do it anywhere—at your desk, on the train, at home, in a rest room—whenever you need a break to refresh body, mind, and soul.

What Is Prayer?

Prayer can—and often does—include what we think of as meditation. Although prayer often means talking to God, it's more effective if you also spend time listening for guidance. Meditation does not deal with specific requests, but prayer sometimes involves petitions for oneself or others ("Please get me out of this mess," or "Please, God, don't let him die"), as well as praise and thanksgiving.

Prayer can be said silently or aloud, alone or in a group. It can be wordless, like meditation, or thick with metaphor and God's presence, like the poetry of the dervish Jalaluddin Rumi or India's poet-saint Mirabai. Like meditation, prayer can be done sitting still or on the move. Moving prayer includes sacred dance, walking a labyrinth, and the ecstatic shaking that gave the Shakers their name.

Though denial or transcendence of the body is historically a part of Eastern and Christian ascetic practices, the body is, in reality, central to prayer life. We are embodied spirit, and our bodies are the vehicles through which we worship and pray. In one important aspect of Christian liturgy—the Eucharist—the body is exalted. In taking communion we symbolically ingest—become one with—the flesh (wafer) and blood (wine) of Christ.

The power of prayer, known intuitively for millennia, is now being demonstrated in the lab. Research finds that our prayers can affect not only ourselves but others, even at a distance and without their knowledge.

What Is Contemplation?

Contemplation has two meanings when it comes to spiritual practice. In the narrow sense it is synonymous with *concentration*—focusing your attention on an object, such as gazing at a sacred image, or reading and musing on a sacred text, as in the practice of Contemplative Prayer.

In the larger sense contemplation is the fruit of all spiritual work. This is the state of "resting in God" that mystics speak of. It can take the form of utter ecstasy, a cosmic embrace, or simply a feeling of being in good hands, of being cradled in the lap of the divine.

Is a Teacher Necessary?

Ask a group of seasoned meditators if a teacher is necessary, and you're likely to hear some unqualified yeses and a few resounding nos. The disagreement is only natural. There is a much longer and stronger tradition of one-on-one spiritual teaching—the guru-student relationship—in the East than in the West. Here, a combination of rugged individualism, mistrust of cults and demagogues, and religious education that discourages direct mystical experience makes us reluctant to put ourselves under the guidance of a spiritual master.

That attitude could be our loss. As Elizabeth Lesser states in *The New American Spirituality:*

> *You do not need a teacher to walk the spiritual path, but you'll get farther along in a more efficient way with one. In many ways the spiritual path is no different from any other learning process, be it music or sports or business. In the beginning it helps to have a teacher—just like it helped to have a piano teacher or a basketball coach when you were young. Even Mozart and Michael Jordan had teachers. A good teacher steeped in a wise and well-developed tradition of personal growth and spiritual transcendence is a blessing.*

Beware, Lesser cautions, of people who have studied with a teacher for years but insist that *you* should be able to do it on your own. "To me," she says, "that is like saying that since music is all around us, all one has to do is sit down at the piano and let it flow out through the fingers onto the keys."

Part of our concern about spiritual teachers stems from our expectations. In spiritual matters we want someone else to do the heavy lifting for us, but at the same time we fear surrendering control. We're missing the point. "The teacher or guru principle manifests as a mirror of our deeper, higher self," Lama Surya Das explains in *Awakening to the Sacred.* "If we are fortunate enough to meet such a fully actualized being, we can see our own potential fulfilled. This is what we can become."

A teacher instructs us in the philosophy and practices of the tradition we choose, and in the East it is thought that there is an actual energy exchange through which the teacher empowers the student. Ultimately, what a teacher does is point us toward truth. "That is the whole art of the teacher," the Sufi master Pir Vilayat explains in *The Call of the Dervish.* "To make you turn your head in the direction of what you are supposed to see."

The other side of working with a teacher or spiritual guide is to make sure we choose one who is worthy of our allegiance. Scandals have rocked a number of spiritual communities in recent decades, as one after another teacher was found to be misusing power. Like psychotherapists, spiritual teachers occupy a delicate position of trust. And they, too, are often recipients of their students' projections. We assume that a spiritual teacher is all knowing, all seeing—and without flaws. Casting ourselves as the humble, ignorant students we may impute more wisdom and judgment to this powerful authority figure than is warranted. Even the most realized teacher is, after all, human.

You should not leave your good sense at the door to the meditation center; it is your responsibility to check the teacher's reputation and credentials. No teacher has a right to exploit a student—sexually, emotionally, or financially—so you are wise to leave immediately if any teacher makes such advances.

The bottom line on teachers is: By all means, look for one. He or she can facilitate your spiritual progress in ways you've never dreamed. At the same time, proceed with caution. The box on page 37 offers Elizabeth Lesser's checklist of what to look for in a teacher and what to avoid.

That said, we turn to the other side of the question: Can you practice without a teacher? The answer is: absolutely. There is a saying in spiritual circles: "Begin where you are." If that means sampling teachings and practices on your own until you find a teacher whose work you admire, then by all means do it. Throughout this book are exercises you can do by yourself, as well as suggestions to fire your imagination and light the spiritual path ahead of you.

For many people, the solo journey—what author and mystic Andrew Harvey calls "the direct path"—is the most appropriate way. Ultimately, each of us is responsible for maintaining our own spiritual commitment and establishing a relationship with the divine, whether or not we study with a teacher. That does not mean, however, that we must travel the spiritual road without the companionship and guidance of "spiritual friends." As explained in Chapter 11, "Creating Community," practicing with like-minded seekers can deepen our spiritual experience, helping us shift from self-centered thinking to awareness that we are members of the community of all beings.

Try This: Finding a Spiritual Teacher

WHAT TO LOOK FOR:

1. *Does she try to walk her talk in the outside world?* The key here is a willingness on the part of the teacher to show some humility, to reveal her struggles, and to attempt to make her life and her message congruent.

2. *Does he demand excellence?* Spirituality practice leads to freedom but requires discipline.

3. *Can you have a regular, how's-the-weather conversation with her?* Look for a teacher who . . . enjoys the fact that we're all in this together.

4. *Is he happy?* Spiritually happy people are kind people. Kindness and compassion are the trademarks of good and great teachers.

5. *Is she experienced?* Has she developed mastery of her subject or tradition?

WHAT TO AVOID:

1. *The "Crazy Wisdom" excuse:* If a teacher and the group around the teacher glibly explain away . . . questionable behavior as "just part of the teachings," take a good, hard look behind the Wizard's curtain.

2. *A lack of boundaries:* A lack of healthy boundaries leads to abusive relationships.

3. *Claims of perfection:* Don't trust a teacher who imperiously claims her own perfection or the superiority of her tradition.

4. *Hiding out:* Some spiritual paths are steeped in such ornate ritual and complex theory that a teacher can hide behind the façade of the tradition. Bring some healthy skepticism along with you whenever you approach a foreign tradition.

—ELIZABETH LESSER, *THE NEW AMERICAN SPIRITUALITY*

RESOURCES

BOOKS

Bandler, Richard, and John Grinder. *Frogs into Princes.* Moab, Ut.: Real People Press, 1979.

The Song of God: Bhagavad-Gita. New York: New American Library, 1972.

Boorstein, Sylvia. *That's Funny, You Don't Look Buddhist.* San Francisco: Harper San Francisco, 1997.

Borysenko, Joan. *The Ways of the Mystic.* Carlsbad, Cal.: Hay House, 1997.

Das, Lama Surya. *Awakening to the Sacred.* New York: Broadway, 1999.

Dass, Ram. *Journey of Awakening.* New York: Bantam, 1978.

Gunaratana, Venerable Henepola. *Mindfulness in Plain English.* Somerville, Mass.: Wisdom, 1991.

Hirsh, Sandra Krebs, and Jane A.G. Kise. *Soul Types.* New York: Hyperion, 1998.

Khan, Pir Vilayat Inayat. *The Call of the Dervish.* Indianapolis: Omega Publications, 1981.

Kornfield, Jack. *A Path with Heart.* New York: Bantam, 1993.

Lesser, Elizabeth. *The New American Spirituality.* New York: Random House, 1999.

Rama, Sri Swami. *Choosing a Path.* Honesdale, Pa.: Himalayan International Institute, 1982.

Richardson, Peter Tufts. *Four Spiritualities.* Palo Alto, Cal.: Davies-Black, 1996.

Sams, Jami. *Dancing the Dream.* San Francisco: Harper San Francisco, 1998.

Simpkinson, Anne A., and Charles H. Simpkinson. *Soul Work.* New York: HarperPerennial, 1998.

WEB SITE

www.pluralism.org

Site of The Pluralism Project at Harvard University, with resources, information, and ongoing research on religious practice in America.

Two

❖

Settling Down

3.
Going Within

Silence is unceasing eloquence.
—RAMANA MAHARSHI

When you think of meditation or contemplation, what is the first word that comes to mind? For most people the word is *silence.* Then, perhaps, *solitude.* Silence and solitude are reasons many people hesitate to try meditation or meditative prayer. Just what will we experience when we sit down by ourselves without the sounds and distractions of people and everyday life?

In *Amazing Grace,* her book of essays on faith, the writer Kathleen Norris tells a story of teaching her young art students about silence as a way to liberate their imaginations. First, she had them make as much noise as possible; then, at a signal, they stopped and sat in absolute stillness. Some students loved the exercise; others were wary. "It's scary," one fifth-grader told Norris. "Why?" she asked. "It's like we're waiting for something," he replied.

That sense of anxious anticipation is common among beginning meditators. Some of us have a sense of what we're waiting for: a glimpse of God; clarity; peace of mind. Others of us, unused to silence, haven't a clue what it holds. What are we so scared of?

In silence we discover our distractedness and obsessive thoughts; our anger, sadness, and disappointment; our unresolved conflicts from the past, concerns about the present, and anxiety about the future. In short, we are confronted with ourselves. Unplugged from telephones, the Internet, and Walkmans, with nothing to listen to and no one to talk to, we hear only our own internal dialogue: *This is ridiculous; Why am I doing this?; My back hurts; My foot's asleep; I'm wasting my time, I have a thousand things to do; This is so boring; Why can't I stop fretting about what so-and-so did to me?* and so on.

Silence, it seems, can be very noisy.

Perhaps what we fear as much as silence is solitude. From childhood we're conditioned to think that spending time alone is wrong—antisocial, even harmful to our mental and physical health. But the issue, suggests Catholic priest Henri J. M. Nouwen in his book on prayer, *With Open Hands*, "is not whether we can live without friends or without feeding our eyes and ears with new impressions—we obviously cannot—but whether we can stand to be alone from time to time, shut our eyes, gently push aside all the assorted noises, and sit calmly and quietly."

In the solitary experience of contemplation we are called on to establish a relationship with that unfamiliar companion, the self. If we are patient and practice sitting with the body still and the breath relaxed, eventually we will find that the internal chatter calms down. Then we can begin to hear the mysteries that silence has to offer.

At first, those mysteries are the mundane sounds of the immediate environment. In day-to-day life we seldom listen closely to what's around us: the call and response of birds, wind through the trees, the whoosh of tires on a rain-slicked street ("The Sounds of Silence," page 43). Once we begin to attend to our surroundings we find that silence brings even greater surprises. Silence and solitude form the medium of self-discovery, in which self-acceptance can take root. The British psychiatrist Anthony Storr argues that being alone is a basic human need—essential to everything from inner growth and confronting loss to creative and spiritual opening. "That solitude promotes insight as well as change has been recognized by great religious leaders, who have usually retreated from the world before returning to it to share what has been revealed to them," Storr writes in *Solitude: A Return to the Self.* Jesus in the wilderness, Muhammad in his cave, the Buddha under the bodhi tree—all reached great awareness in silence.

Silence and solitude are the direct route to our "real" self, our deepest spiritual core. When the body and breath and thoughts are still, silence becomes palpable, like a giant sigh of relief. "Ahhhh," your whole being seems to say. In that moment of release—sometimes called *samadhi*—you feel a deep contentment, as if you have come home to yourself.

In many monasteries and contemplative communities silence is the order of the day. It is the background texture of daily life, the context for making mundane existence into an ongoing meditation or prayer. In Buddhist retreats there is a tradition called the Noble Silence. This means that for the duration of the retreat—anywhere from a few days to a few years—there is no communication between participants, not even eye contact or sign language, and no reading, writing, radio, or TV. The effect of this total silence is electric: you become aware of every nuance of sensation, down to the flow of energy through your subtle-body system. Even the mind gives up its protesting and relaxes into a kind of limpid ease.

What becomes apparent then is that true silence is not noiselessness but spaciousness. As the Zen master Dainin Katagiri Roshi points out in *Returning to Silence,* this spacious no-sound "is a vastness from which your capacity, your knowledge, your nature, comes, just like spring water coming up from the earth." Silence makes space for spirit.

Making Friends with Silence

Since silence seems to be the source of great spiritual riches, how do we make friends with it? The way, the sages tell us, is just to begin.

Being in silence is like being in the dark: at first you may feel apprehensive. But just as you might sit quietly in the dark until your eyes adjusted, if you sit awhile in silence you'll begin to feel at ease. The exercise "Being in Silence" (below) shows how to create a sense of safety and privacy that will allow you to relax into the spaciousness of silence.

Lama Surya Das, an American-born Tibetan Buddhist teacher, suggests making

Try This: Being in Silence

Find a quiet place, close the door, turn off the TV, radio, CD/cassette player, and phone. Sit comfortably on a cushion or in a chair with your arms resting at your sides. Close your eyes. Become aware of your breathing. Feel the rising and falling of your breath in your belly. As your breathing becomes smoother, focus on your body. Does it feel tense anywhere? Gently release the tightness.

Let yourself become aware of your surroundings. What do you hear? Is there a dog barking, a clock ticking, the hum of traffic outside? What do you feel? Is the air warm or cold? Are you bored or afraid? If fear comes up, imagine you are breathing into it, releasing it. If you are still afraid, open your eyes and gaze with a soft focus at a spot on the floor about four or five feet in front of you. Continue breathing gently for another five or ten minutes, remaining open to your surroundings without focusing on anything in particular. As you become more comfortable in silence, add five minutes each day to this exercise until you reach thirty minutes a session.

After you have finished, you may want to write a brief entry in your journal describing your experience. Later, you will be able to look back on these entries and see how your early fears and doubts diminished as you developed a relationship with yourself in silence and solitude.

silent retreat a part of your ordinary life, even if only for a few hours now and then ("Noble Silence," page 46). This practice, he writes in *Awakening the Buddha Within*, "is an excellent way to quiet our habitual busy bodies and overactive rational minds while becoming more receptive, self-reflective, and sensitive." People who regularly observe a day or afternoon of silence and solitude report that it helps them balance and focus their lives and approach problems more creatively.

Spiritual writings in nearly every tradition refer to the power of silence to reveal truth. It was in silence that Elijah heard the "still small voice" of God—and in silence that centuries of Eastern and Western mystics have received guidance.

Many teachers tout the eloquence of silence. "The truth does not have to utter a word; it is just there," Pir Vilayat writes in *The Call of the Dervish*. Sri Ramana Maharshi, one of the great sages of modern India (he died in 1950), occasionally gave oral teachings but insisted that silence carried more force. "Deep meditation is eternal speech," he said. "Silent initiation changes the hearts of all."

In *Awakening the Buddha Within* Surya Das tells us, "Silence is the song of the heart, like love, a universal language, a natural melody open to anyone, even the tone deaf or religiously challenged. Try going out into the woods or sitting very near the ocean's waves. Look up at the bright stars at night; open your mind's inner ear and listen to the lovely song of silence."

From this bucolic bliss it is only a short step back inside to your meditation cushion. Here, more dimensions of silence will unfold. The song may become more like a chorus, a cacophony of voices with at least one voice trying to convince you that meditation isn't worth the bother. Ignore it. Make a commitment to stay with your meditation for at least a week or two. By then chances are you will have begun to sense the wisdom in it.

Having made friends with silence, you can approach meditation and prayer with a sense of anticipation: What will I learn? What will my thoughts reveal to me? What will I hear if I really listen?

Silence, Henri Nouwen suggests, "offers the freedom to stroll in your own inner yard, and to rake up the leaves there and clear the paths so you can easily find the way to your heart. Perhaps there will be much fear and uncertainty when you first come upon this 'unfamiliar terrain,' but slowly and surely you will discover an order and a

Try This: Noble Silence

Why not take a Sunday off, or half a day, to be by yourself . . . and experience for yourself the unspeakable joy and virtue in Noble Silence? Spend the time in your room, house, or garden without using any communication devices. Or spend your time alone in nature, communing with yourself. You'll love it.

Stop.
Be still.
Remain silent.
Meditators should be seen,
not heard.
Ssshhh.
Still
All the senses.
Let everything be.
Let go, and let it all
come to you.
Relax.
Being is in;
doing is out.
Do nothing.
For a moment
Just be.
Silence
is
golden.
Enjoy it.

—LAMA SURYA DAS, *AWAKENING THE BUDDHA WITHIN*

familiarity which deepens your longing to stay home." (If your fear is great, try the "Breathing in the Heart" exercise above.)

There is something else essential that emerges from silence, Nouwen points out: it allows us to recognize that the urge to get up from our cushions and do anything *but* meditate is a sure sign that we're still looking outside ourselves for what can only be found within. Self-awareness is an inevitable result of meditating. Sometimes a desire for more self-knowledge is all it takes to make a commitment to try meditation or prayer. Whatever practice you choose, you're more likely to stick with it if its benefits are clear.

Calm Mind, Healthy Body

A calm mind and healthy body are scientifically demonstrated benefits of regular meditation and prayer. Groundbreaking research at Harvard Medical School by cardiologist Herbert Benson showed that meditation can lower blood pressure—the now-famous "relaxation response." This is just one example of how mind/body changes associated with meditation and prayer directly affect health. *In Healing Words: The Power of Prayer and the Practice of Medicine,* physician Larry Dossey describes a number of studies showing that prayer can facilitate healing even when the petitions are delivered at a distance, without the patient's knowledge.

Increasingly, doctors and other health professionals are prescribing meditation instead of medication to relieve stress that can lead to illness. Most of these techniques are drawn directly from time-tested ancient spiritual practices. Psychologist Jon Kabat-Zinn's innovative program for the Stress Reduction Clinic at the University of Massachusetts Medical Center incorporates hatha yoga and mindfulness, a technique of moment-to-moment, nonjudgmental awareness based on a practice used 2,500 years ago by the Buddha (see Chapter 5).

Extensive research with Transcendental Meditation (TM) practitioners and other spiritual adepts shows that meditation can boost energy; speed recovery from surgery

---

Inspiration: *The Healing Power of Awareness*

When something goes wrong with our body or our mind, we have the natural expectation that medicine can make it right, and often it can. But . . . our active collaboration is essential in almost all forms of medical therapy. It is particularly vital in the case of chronic diseases and conditions for which medicine has no cures. In such cases the quality of your life may greatly depend on your own ability to know your body and mind well enough to work at optimizing your own health. . . . [Meditation practice] catalyzes the work of healing.

—JON KABAT-ZINN, *FULL CATASTROPHE LIVING*

or injury; relieve asthma, drug abuse, and other chronic conditions—and, as thousands of athletes have discovered, improve chances of a winning performance.

Becoming Aware

You don't need to be ailing—or athletic—to find meditation or meditative prayer life-changing, however. Sitting in silence, reaching a relaxed and open state, transforms the mind, improving clarity, flexibility, concentration, and memory. Hundreds of studies corroborate what meditators have long known: that meditation helps us become more peaceful, centered, and aware.

Paradoxically, as we become more self-reflective, we become more, rather than less, responsive to the outside world. Researchers in Japan found that even while in deep meditation, Zen monks maintained full awareness of lights and sounds around them.

With continued practice the attentive state reached in meditation carries over into daily life. Meditation improves resiliency, the ability to roll with the punches. Life

Try This: Being with Dissatisfaction

The next time you feel a sense of dissatisfaction, of something being missing or not quite right, turn inward just as an experiment. See if you can capture the energy of that very moment. Instead of picking up a magazine or going to the movies, calling a friend or looking for something to eat or acting up in one way or another, make a place for yourself. Sit down and enter into your breathing, if only for a few minutes. Don't look for anything—neither flowers nor light nor a beautiful view. Don't extol the virtues of anything or condemn the inadequacy of anything. Don't even think to yourself, *I am going inward now.* Just sit. Reside at the center of the world. Let things be as they are.

—JON KABAT-ZINN, *WHEREVER YOU GO, THERE YOU ARE*

won't stop coming at you, but you'll be better able to deal with situations as they arise and to bounce back from disappointments.

Despite the obvious benefits of meditation some people balk at trying it. For a take-charge Westerner it may seem too passive—just "navel-gazing." Perhaps family or friends disparage the practice, arguing that self-examination is a way of avoiding day-to-day commitments or obligations to others.

How ironic when, in fact, meditation makes us less, rather than more, self-absorbed. As we descend into silence and experience the spaciousness within, the boundaries between "inside" and "outside," "self" and "other," start to blur. An inevitable consequence of meditation and prayer is experiencing a greater sense of empathy, of connection to other people and unity with all existence. That doesn't make us saints, by any means, but it becomes easier to step back and remember that we're all fellow beings with the same essential needs.

Spiritual Rewards

Above all, the benefit of silence and solitude is spiritual. As Surya Das explains, "True inner silence puts you in touch with the deeper dimensions of being and knowing."

In *Gifts of the Spirit* co-author Philip Zaleski describes a time when he was rock-climbing as a boy and momentarily lost his footing. Frozen to the side of the cliff, he frantically begged God for help until, he recalls, "something—to this day, I don't know what—told me that this was the wrong way to proceed. I stopped whining and began, in silence, to say the Lord's Prayer. A great stillness entered my body. I finished the prayer and began to ascend."

Prayer, meditation, and contemplation are not guaranteed to save our lives, bring us love or riches, or restore our health. But an honest willingness to give these practices a fair trial will produce results beyond our imagining, enabling us to maintain inner peace in the midst of turmoil and become beacons of sanity in the world around us. This is the way of the everyday mystic. We'll learn more about this path in subsequent chapters.

There are many definitions of "mystic" and "mysticism." One of the clearest comes from *Practical Mysticism*, British poet Evelyn Underhill's 1915 classic: "Mysticism is the art of union with Reality. The mystic is a person who has attained that union in greater or less degree, or who aims at and believes in such attainment." To psychologist Lawrence LeShan, author of one of the best basic books on meditation, *How to Meditate*, a mystic is one who "has this knowledge as background music to his daily experience or . . . works consistently to attain this knowledge."

Mystical experience encompasses everything from the most dramatic, paradigm-shattering confrontation with the holy to a brief glimpse of the sacred when we see love flicker in another's eyes.

Begin Now

What, then, is the first step on the contemplative path? How, exactly, should we begin meditation or meditative prayer? You do not need to go off to a monastery or retreat center—though that can be helpful (see Chapter 11: "Creating Community"). You do not need to wait for the right day, the right mood, the right weather, enough money, or the right clothes. Just pull up a chair or meditation cushion and sit down.

There are a number of good books with techniques to get you started, listed in the Resources section on page 52. (For a detailed exploration of meditative prayer, see Chapter 7, page 105.) If you have never meditated, one easy way is to count breaths. A basic practice involves silently counting each exhalation from one to ten, then starting again. (You may find it easier to count from one to four, as Lawrence LeShan suggests.) When you find your mind wandering (*What, I can't even count to ten without daydreaming?* you chide yourself), rest assured that this happens to everyone. Simply stop, gently turn your attention back to counting, and begin again at one.

This exercise teaches concentration—basic to meditation, contemplation, and prayer. Contemplative practices are, above all, ongoing lessons in attention. Or, as the great teachers tell us, in bringing the mind back home.

Simple, but Not Easy

Except for very advanced or esoteric practices, meditation techniques are not complicated. What is difficult is mastering your mind. Often, in spiritual writings, the untamed mind is compared to an unfettered animal—a galloping horse, say, or a chattering monkey. In the modern classic *Zen Mind, Beginner's Mind* the Japanese Zen teacher Shunryu Suzuki Roshi uses the metaphor of a sheep or cow.

> *To give your sheep or cow a large, spacious meadow is a way to control him. So it is with people: first let them do what they want, and watch them . . . without trying to control them. The same way works for yourself. . . . If you want to obtain perfect calmness in your zazen, you should not be bothered by the various images you find in your mind. Let them come, and let them go. Then they will be under control. But this policy is not so easy. It sounds easy, but it requires some special effort. How to make this kind of effort is the secret of practice.*

Throughout this book you will be introduced to exercises and techniques drawn from many traditions, so that you can find the one that most suits you. As we pointed out in Chapter 2, "Getting Ready," what is most important in setting out on a spiritual journey is to find a path—a practice—that resonates with your heart, your deepest longing. Then, even when the way seems hard, you will be able to turn to the simple form you have chosen and, in silence and solitude, return to the Source.

✍   RESOURCES   ✍

BOOKS

Benson, Herbert, M.D., and Miriam Z. Klipper. *The Relaxation Response.* New York: Avon, 1990.

Benson, Herbert, M.D., and William Proctor. *Beyond the Relaxation Response.* New York: Berkeley, 1994.

Das, Lama Surya. *Awakening the Buddha Within.* New York: Broadway, 1997.

Dass, Ram. *Be Here Now.* New York: Crown, 1971.

————. *Journey of Awakening.* New York: Bantam, 1978.

————. *Miracle of Love: Stories About Neem Karoli Baba.* San Anselmo, Cal.: Hanuman Foundation, 1979.

Dossey, Larry, M.D. *Healing Words.* San Francisco: Harper San Francisco, 1993.

Goodman, David, ed. *Be as You Are: The Teachings of Sri Ramana Maharshi.* New York: Penguin Arkana, 1985.

Kabat-Zinn, Jon. *Full Catastrophe Living.* New York: Delta, 1990.

————. *Wherever You Go, There You Are.* New York: Hyperion, 1994.

Katagiri, Dainin. *Returning to Silence.* Boston: Shambhala, 1988.

Khan, Pir Vilayat Inayat. *The Call of the Dervish.* Indianapolis: Omega Publications, 1991.

LeShan, Lawrence. *How to Meditate.* New York: Back Bay, 1999.

Maharshi, Ramana. *The Spiritual Teaching of Ramana Maharshi.* Boston: Shambhala, 1988.

Merton, Thomas. *The Wisdom of the Desert.* New York: New Directions, 1960.

Murphy, Michael, and Steven Donovan. *The Physical and Psychological Effects of Meditation.* Sausalito, Cal.: Institute of Noetic Sciences, 1997.

Norris, Kathleen. *Amazing Grace.* New York: Riverhead, 1998.

Nouwen, Henri J.M. *With Open Hands.* New York: Ballantine, 1972.

————. *With Open Hands,* illustrated. Notre Dame, Ind.: Ave Maria Press, 1995.

Osho. *Meditation: The First and Last Freedom.* New York: St. Martin's Griffin, 1996.

Storr, Anthony. *Solitude: A Return to the Self.* New York: Ballantine, 1988.

Suzuki, Shunryu. *Zen Mind, Beginner's Mind.* New York: Weatherhill, 1970.

Underhill, Evelyn. *Practical Mysticism.* New York: Dutton, 1915.

Zaleski, Philip, and Paul Kaufman. *Gifts of the Spirit.* San Francisco: Harper San Francisco, 1997.

WEB SITE

www.tm.org

Web site of the Transcendental Meditation (TM) program, with information on the technique and how to find a teacher.

4.

Finding
Stillness

Why do we meditate? Different people offer very different answers. Your doctor might suggest meditating to help you lower your blood pressure or handle stress better. Your boss or your best friend might suggest it to help you control your temper. You might be going through a period of great suffering or personal crisis and look to meditation for solace. Or perhaps it's just the opposite: everything is going along fine—too fine—and you wonder if there isn't more to living. You want to go deeper, to find answers to fundamental questions about the purpose of life, of *your* life—to find a connection to the very ground of being.

On a practical level meditation is an efficient way to quiet the mind and observe the way it works. In that sense meditation is a kind of technology—a means to see clearly our mental meandering: the obsessive thinking, worrying, fretting, and ambivalence; the pain of our internal dramas, our personal stories.

Enlightenment is often described as a great stillness of the mind, in which we realize our own true nature and our unity with all being. This does not mean that all thought stops. Rather, it means that the awakened mind drops its opinions and judgments and conceptions—all those ideas and assumptions we cling to that separate us from one another. The Japanese Zen master Yasutani Roshi, in a lecture recounted in *The Three Pillars of Zen*, explains that meditation practice "does not aim at rendering the mind inactive but at quieting and unifying it in the midst of activity."

Meditation grounds us in reality. It helps us create an intimate relationship with ourselves. How often we've heard it said that until we love and accept ourselves we cannot truly love and accept others or see ourselves as part of the community of all beings. Practiced diligently, meditation can lead us to a clearer understanding of—and compassion for—all of life.

Even though meditation improves physical and mental health, it is at bottom not a therapy but a spiritual practice. "Peace and joy is our goal," the Hindu teacher Sri Swami Satchidananda explains in *Beyond Words*. "Not everyone believes in a god. But the real God, the absolute God, the cosmic God who is being searched for by one and all, is that peace and joy."

So, how do we find peace and joy? "Be still and know that I am God," Psalm 46 tells us. It is in stillness that we begin to get a glimpse of the kingdom where peace and joy reside. In the previous chapter we spoke of silence and solitude. They create the context—the container—for holding the inner stillness and spaciousness in which we can discover the sacred.

Sit Down in the Heart of the Matter

Something in us knows the way. Bhante Wimala, a Buddhist monk from Sri Lanka who is a resident teacher at Omega Institute, writes in *Lessons of the Lotus*, "I am convinced human beings are provided with the foundation and potential necessary for spiritual growth and awakening. It is our birthright." A woman who has been meditating for twenty years recalls a vision she had some months before she sat for the first time. At that point her life was in chaos, and despite years of psychotherapy she feared she would never experience peace of mind or any sort of equanimity. One evening, while she was ruminating on her distress, the image of a wall suddenly flashed across her mind.

> *I somehow knew without doubt that the wall was what separated me from a sense of connection—to inner peace, or a higher power, or even to my deepest self. An inner voice told me that no matter what I tried, I could neither go over the wall nor under it nor around it. I felt total despair. Then the idea popped into my head that I had no choice but to sit in front of the wall and that at some point, it would dissolve, and on the other side I would find the peace and clarity I sought. Shortly after that experience someone told me about a Zen center only a block from my house. I knew nothing about Zen meditation, but I went inside. I was instructed to sit down on a cushion facing a blank white wall. In that moment I realized the meaning of my vision. I sensed that Zen practice would lead me to some kind of inner liberation.*

As this woman's experience shows, you don't need to know your destination to begin meditating. You only need to start down the path. One of the first steps is to create the time and space for spiritual practice.

Creating Sacred Space

Most of what you need for meditation you already possess—willingness, breath, an inner yearning. But you will also need a place to sit. Meditating with a group can be very supportive (see Chapter 11: "Creating Community"); however, it is also good to have a spot where you can practice on your own. Like exercise, meditation requires discipline and consistency; you are more likely to do it if you have a special place that is convenient and welcoming and feels like sacred space.

What makes a space sacred is a matter of individual preference. One meditator used the occasion of moving to a new home to define her idea of it:

> I had no furniture at all for the living room, so for several months it was bare while I tried to figure out how to decorate it. Then I read somewhere that traditional Persian dwellings had something called a "nothing room": it was deliberately kept empty to leave room for spirit. I decided that's what I wanted. The only things I put in my nothing room were two ficus trees, a small altar, and a meditation cushion. It felt like holy ground.

You do not need a whole room devoted to meditation or contemplation. The area can be no more than a small corner, as long as it is clean and quiet and you can sit there undisturbed. You can mark the space as sacred by organizing it around an altar. Altars are an ancient focus for worship. In fact, we build altars all the time, without thinking of it, creating arrangements of beloved objects or good-luck charms on tabletops, mantels, desks—even on our computers.

You can create a simple altar on a small table or any flat surface and decorate it with a candle, incense, fresh flowers, and objects that are precious to you—perhaps a special stone or crystal, a feather or a shell, talismans, an image of a deity or teacher you admire. You might want a little bell or gong you can ring to mark the beginning and end of your meditation. Lighting a candle before you start and extinguishing it when you finish is another way to acknowledge the reverence of the time you have set aside for spiritual practice.

As your practice deepens, your altar may assume more significance. In *A Place of Your Own*, his guide to creating a personal meditation space, Edward Searl recalls: "Within the first six months of exploring the place of my own that was my altar, I found that it had become indispensable to my spiritual life. It was a refuge and a place of comfort."

Near your altar you might want to keep a few inspirational books. Some people like to read a passage or two before meditating. Keep a journal and pen close by, so that at the end of your meditation period you can write down any observations or questions about your practice that arise. This will serve as an ongoing record of your journey. Later on, if you feel discouraged about your progress, a glance at your journal will show you how far you've come.

Posture

It is, of course, possible to meditate in any position, even lying down. But concentration and breathing will be easier—and you are less likely to fall asleep—if you sit comfortably with your back straight, your head erect, and your chin tucked in slightly. If you imagine that an invisible string connects the crown of your head to the heavens, your head and spine will naturally come into alignment.

Most meditators sit on a firm round cushion (called a *zafu* in Japanese) placed on the floor. For comfort you can set the cushion on top of a rug or folded blanket or square mat (a *zabuton*). To find out where to order meditation cushions, see "Meditation Supplies," page 67.

In Eastern meditative practices it is traditional to sit cross-legged in what is known as the lotus position. *Full lotus* means sitting with both legs crossed and each foot resting on the opposite thigh. Unless you are naturally very flexible or have much experience at meditating, this posture may be uncomfortable or difficult to assume. Alternatively, you can sit with just one foot resting on the opposite thigh (half lotus) or on the opposite calf (quarter lotus). Some people find the Burmese position easier: Sitting on the cushion, bend your right knee and bring your right foot close to your crotch. Bend your left knee and bring your left foot close to your body, in front of the right foot.

If you prefer, you can kneel, resting your buttocks on a small meditation bench or cushion, or straddling a cushion placed between your knees. If neither floor-sitting nor kneeling works for you, it's fine to use a chair. The chair should be straight enough to allow you to sit erect and the right height so you can place both feet firmly on the ground.

Whatever posture you choose, make sure you feel stable and balanced so you can sit quietly without moving. Unless you are in excruciating pain, try not to adjust your position during your meditation period. Dealing with discomfort is one of the lessons of meditating. Observing our pain as it comes and goes teaches us about impermanence: everything passes.

Maintaining posture is a key element of practice. "The most important point is to own your own physical body," the Zen teacher Shunryu Suzuki Roshi advises in *Zen Mind, Beginner's Mind.* "If you slump, you will lose yourself. Your mind will be wandering about somewhere else; you will not be in your body." (During a Zen retreat you may hear the meditation leader shout, "Don't move!" This is to encourage, not punish.)

Hand positions or gestures (known as *mudras*) have great significance in several traditions, but in the beginning it is best to keep them simple. A common way to hold the hands for meditation is to rest them lightly on the thighs, palms down, with the fingers outstretched or forming a circle with the thumb and forefinger. Zen meditators generally place their hands in the lap, palms up, with the left hand cradled in the right and the thumbs touching to create an oval. You can also rest your hands in your lap with the right hand lightly grasping the left thumb.

Paying Attention

Meditation promotes inner vision. So it's natural to wonder: Should you meditate with eyes open or closed? That depends on preference and which method you choose.

Zazen, the practice of Zen Buddhism, is done with eyes half opened, the gaze softened and directed slightly downward at the floor or at a blank wall a few feet in front of you. Other schools of meditation generally opt for eyes closed.

One longtime meditator remembers that when she first started sitting, she was afraid to close her eyes. "From childhood I'd been one of those hypervigilant types," she says. "It took me a while before I realized that what I feared most was not an outside attack but my own inner demons."

Meditating with your eyes slightly open helps you stay alert and focused on your practice, rather than on visions that may arise. (In Zen those visions are called *makyo*— "little devils" that tempt you off the path.) On the other hand, closing your eyes reduces outside distractions. Either way, being alert is the goal. "Meditation is simply a quiet, effortless, one-pointed focus of attention and awareness," the Indian yogi Swami Rama points out in *Meditation and Its Practice*.

What are you paying attention to? In Chapter 3, "Going Within," we suggested a basic meditation focused on breathing—counting breaths. (Other breathing exercises

Try This: Sensing, Looking, and Listening

Step 1: Sensing your body. Seat yourself in a comfortable chair. Close your eyes. Sense whatever you are aware of in your body, starting from the top of your head and proceeding down to your feet. Notice sensations, temperature, tension, emotions, energy, movement, and so on—including no feeling or sensation. What is your overall sense of yourself when you finish?

Step 2: Looking and listening. Open your eyes and bring your attention to the experience of looking and listening. Pay more attention to the overall experience of looking— seeing patterns, colors, and shapes, than to anything in particular you are seeing. Do the same with listening. Be aware of yourself as someone who is looking and listening. These are two of your most common activities, but normally, you focus on what you perceive and not on the experiencing of looking and listening itself.

—ADAPTED FROM *SOUL WITHOUT SHAME* BY BYRON BROWN

follow in this chapter.) Alternatively, you could focus on your body and your surroundings. It is easier to be aware of physical sensations and the immediate environment when you're sitting quietly. And like all meditation practices this one ultimately leads to greater awareness in everyday life. In the Diamond Approach, a spiritual path based on timeless wisdom and psychological insight taught by Hameed Ali, who writes under the name A. H. Almaas, there is a practice called "Sensing, Looking, and Listening" that hones attentiveness and "self-remembering"—being fully conscious of your experience in any moment (see page 60).

Breathing

Just as breath is the essence of life, it is at the very heart of meditation (see "Breathe," page 62). We all breathe, all the time, without fail. So, what a perfect object of contemplation breathing is!

Pranayama, or breath awareness, is central to yoga practice (*prana* means "breath" in Sanskrit). Advanced yogis aspire to great feats of breath control, but every mystical tradition emphasizes breathing to relax the body, still the mind, and bring our attention back to the present moment. As the beloved Vietnamese Zen master Thich Nhat Hanh explains in *The Miracle of Mindfulness,* "breath is the bridge which connects life to consciousness, which unites your body to your thoughts. Whenever your mind becomes scattered, use your breath as the means to take hold of your mind again."

Under stress, breathing becomes shallow or erratic. When we're tense, we may hold ourselves so tightly, we forget to exhale. When we're afraid, we may gulp air or hyperventilate. In meditation we learn not to hold the breath or force it but to take deep, relaxed inhalations followed by long, slow exhalations. Breathing correctly increases the flow of oxygen to the body and the brain, giving us more energy and sharpening our awareness. The very rhythm of life—and meditation practice—is borne on the rise and fall of the breath.

Deep, diaphragmatic breathing is basic to many meditations. It is sometimes called three-part breathing because each inhalation involves three steps: drawing the breath in through the nostrils, sending it down into the chest, and then into the abdomen. This type of breathing is very grounding, anchoring your concentration in the *hara*—a point approximately two finger-widths below the navel, which in the Hindu and Buddhist traditions is viewed as the vital energy center of the body, "the seat of the soul."

To learn three-part breathing, Swami Rama suggests lying on your back with your upper arms at your sides. With your elbows bent, rest one hand lightly on your upper chest, the other on your diaphragm. You can then feel the movement as your chest and abdomen rise with each inhalation and lower as you exhale.

There are many ways to meditate on breathing. Some involve simply "watching" the breath, with or without counting. The *Anapanasati Sutta*—the *Sutta of the Full Awareness of Breathing*—outlines the Buddha's teachings on conscious breathing as a foundation for mindfulness and spiritual awakening. In *Breathe! You Are Alive*, Thich Nhat Hanh offers a series of exercises based on the Buddha's method. Sitting in a quiet place, with

Inspiration: Breathe

Breathe.
Breathe again.
Smile.
Relax.
Arrive
Where you are.
Be natural.
Open to effortlessness,
To being
Rather than doing.
Drop everything.
Let go.
Enjoy for a moment
This marvelous joy of meditation.

—LAMA SURYA DAS, *AWAKENING THE BUDDHA WITHIN*

your back erect, focus on following the breath as you think: *Breathing in, I know I am breathing in. Breathing out, I know I am breathing out.* Continue, shifting the focus slightly to "Breathing in, my breath goes deep. Breathing out, my breath goes slow." Move on to "Breathing in, I am aware of my whole body," then "Breathing out, I calm my whole body." Next, "Breathing in, I know I am alive. Breathing out, I feel the joy of being alive." Like the Sensing, Looking, and Listening practice, concentrating on breathing helps us become calm and aware.

Thich Nhat Hanh also suggests ways to pay attention to the breath while you are going about the business of life. One example is "Following Your Breath While Listening to Music" (see below). Another is a lovely mantra—sacred verse—that you can repeat silently throughout the day, whether you are walking, running, washing the dishes, or sitting in meditation:

Breathing in, I calm my body.
Breathing out, I smile.
Dwelling in the present moment,
I know this is a wonderful moment.

Observing the breath may seem simple, but it takes patience and diligence to develop the discipline to return to the breath whenever your attention wanders—and to return to your meditation cushion whenever your resolve falters. Over time the discipline will come.

Try This: Following Your Breath While Listening to Music

Listen to a piece of music. Breathe long, light, and even breaths. Follow your breath, be master of it while remaining aware of the movement and sentiments of the music. Do not get lost in the music, but continue to be master of your breath and your self.

—THICH NHAT HANH, *THE MIRACLE OF MINDFULNESS*

Making a Commitment

Everyone asks when, and for how long, it is advisable to meditate. Is it better to sit in the morning or the evening? Once or twice a day? Is it necessary to sit every day? How long should the meditation period be?

In formal retreats sitting periods are generally anywhere from thirty minutes to an hour in length. It takes even experienced meditators five to ten minutes to settle down into a smooth breathing pattern and a steady practice, so if you only allow that much time for meditating, you will not go very deep. When you are just learning to meditate, it's okay to start with ten minutes—or less, if that's all the concentration you can muster. But try to add five minutes to your sitting period every day or every other day until you reach at least half an hour.

More important than how long you meditate is that you do it regularly, most teachers emphasize. Spiritual practice is about showing up and sitting on the cushion, as meditation teacher Sharon Salzberg puts it. Daily practice helps you strengthen not only your spiritual resolve but your commitment to yourself and your life in general.

Setting aside a regular time for practice also helps you maintain your commitment. Whether you meditate in the morning or the evening or both is a matter of personal preference. Many people like to meditate on arising, when the mind is fresh. That way you can start the rest of your day on a calm note. If you prefer to exercise or do yoga in the morning, early evening is another good time to meditate. It helps you unwind and gain energy for the evening ahead. Meditating right before bed is generally not advised, as it may make you too alert to sleep.

Sometimes, finding time to meditate seems impossible: you would have to get up too early; you have too many family obligations in the morning; you come home too late at the end of the day; you have to cook dinner and put the kids to bed. These are all legitimate concerns, but if you truly want to practice, you will find time somewhere in your schedule. And after you've been practicing awhile, you will realize an age-old truth: that time invested in meditation comes back to you threefold—in more focused and efficient use of your time, in a deepening spiritual connection, and in a healthier, happier life.

BOOKS

Almaas, A. H. *Essence: The Diamond Approach to Inner Realization.* York Beach, Me.: Samuel Weiser, 1986.

———. *Diamond Heart, Books I–IV.* Berkeley: Diamond Books, 1987–97.

Bodri, William, and Lee Shu-Mei. *Twenty-Five Doors to Meditation.* York Beach, Me.: Samuel Weiser, 1998.

Brown, Byron. *Soul Without Shame.* Boston: Shambhala, 1999.

Carrington, Patricia. *The Book of Meditation.* Boston: Element, 1998.

———. *Learn to Meditate Kit.* Boston: Element, 1998.

Cooper, David A. *A Heart of Stillness.* Woodstock, Vt.: Skylight Paths, 1999.

Das, Lama Surya. *Awakening the Buddha Within.* New York: Broadway, 1997.

———. *Awakening to the Sacred.* New York: Broadway, 1999.

Davich, Victor N. *The Best Guide to Meditation.* Los Angeles: Renaissance, 1998.

Fontana, David. *The Elements of Meditation.* Boston: Element, 1991.

———. *Learn to Meditate.* San Francisco: Chronicle Books, 1999.

———. *The Meditator's Handbook.* Boston: Element, 1998.

George, Mike. *Learn to Relax.* San Francisco: Chronicle Books, 1998.

Kapleau, Philip, ed. *The Three Pillars of Zen.* Boston: Beacon Press, 1965.

Khema, Ayya. *Who Is My Self? A Guide to Buddhist Meditation.* Omaha: Wisdom Publications, 1997.

Linn, Denise. *Altars.* New York: Ballantine Wellspring, 1999.

Nhat Hahn, Thich. *Breathe! You Are Alive.* Berkeley: Parallax Press, 1996.

———. *The Miracle of Mindfulness.* Boston: Beacon Press, 1975.

Rama, Swami. *Meditation and Its Practice.* Honesdale, Pa.: Himalayan Institute Press, 1992.

Rama, Swami; Rudolph Ballentine, M.D., and Alan Hymes, M.D. *Science of Breath.* Honesdale, Pa.: Himalayan Institute Press, 1998.

Salzberg, Sharon. *A Heart as Wide as the World.* Boston: Shambhala, 1997.

Satchidananda, Sri Swami. *Beyond Words.* Buckingham, Va.: Integral Yoga, 1992.

Searl, Edward. *A Place of Your Own.* New York: Berkeley, 1998.

Smith, Jean. *Breath Sweeps Mind.* New York: Riverhead, 1998.

Starr, Anthony. *Solitude: A Return to the Self.* New York: Ballantine, 1988.

Suzuki, Shunryu. *Zen Mind, Beginner's Mind.* New York: Weatherhill, 1970.

Titmuss, Christopher. *The Power of Meditation.* New York: Sterling, 1999 (with CD).

Trungpa, Chögyam. *Meditation in Action.* Boston: Shambhala, 1969.

————. *The Myth of Freedom.* Boston: Shambhala, 1976.

Wimala, Bhante Y. *Lessons of the Lotus.* New York: Bantam Books, 1997.

PERIODICALS

Tricycle: The Buddhist Review
92 Van Dam Street #3
New York, NY 10013
(212) 645–1143
quarterly

Parabola
656 Broadway Suite 615
New York, NY 10012
(212) 505–6200
quarterly

AUDIO/VIDEO

Alan Watts Teaches Meditation. Alan W. Watts. One of the West's most respected authorities on Buddhist teaching and practice (Audio Renaissance).

The Art of Meditation. Daniel Goleman, PhD. Classic meditation techniques to calm the body, quiet the mind, improve concentration, and strengthen the immune system (Audio Renaissance).

Beginner's Guide to Meditation. Joan Borysenko. Basic instruction on many different meditation styles (Hay House).

Breathing as a Metaphor for Living. Dennis Lewis. Teachings and exercises on complete and natural breathing (Sounds True).

Global Meditation. Four-cassette set with thirty-page booklet of meditation methods, traditional chants, and spiritual songs from around the world. A portion of sales goes to global aid organizations (Company Relaxation).

Sky Above, Earth Below. John P. Milton. A course on meditating in nature (Sounds True).

MEDITATION SUPPLIES

Carolina Morning Designs
PO Box 509
Micaville, NC 28755
(828) 675–0490
www.zafu.net
Meditation cushions, benches

DharmaCrafts
405 Waltham Street Suite 234
Lexington, MA 02421
(800) 794–9862
Meditation cushions and benches, bells and gongs, incense and burners, prayer beads,
    statues.

Samadhi Cushions
30 Church Street
Barnet, VT 05821
(802) 633–4440
www.samadhicushions.com
gomden, zafu, zabuton mat, support cushions.

Shasta Abbey
3724 Summit Drive
Mount Shasta, CA 96067
(800) 653–3315
Buddhist meditation supplies, including gongs, temple instruments, incense, cushions,
    benches.

Traditional Malas (Prayer Beads):
Chöpa Imports
PO Box 21516
Boulder, CO 80308
(800) 961–2555
info@chopa.com

Contemporary Prayer Beads:
Eleanor Wiley
1402 Santa Clara Avenue
Alameda, CA 94501
(510) 865–7540
prayerbdzs@aol.com

CENTERS
Cambridge Insight Meditation Center
331 Broadway
Cambridge, MA 02139
(617) 441–9038 / (617) 491–5070

Dhamma Dena
HC-1 Box 250
Joshua Tree, CA 92252
(760) 362–4815

Naropa University
2130 Arapahoe Avenue
Boulder, CO 80302
(800) 772–6951

Northwest Dharma Association
305 Harrison Street
Seattle, WA 98109
(206) 441–6811

Southern Dharma Retreat Center
1661 West Road
Hot Springs, NC 28743
(828) 622–7112

Spirit Rock Meditation Center
PO Box 909
Woodacre, CA 94973
(415) 488–0164 / 0170

WEB SITE
www.naropa.edu
Information on academic programs offered by Naropa University (see above)

5.

Mindfulness

Mindfulness provides a simple but powerful
route for getting ourselves unstuck, back [in]
touch with our own wisdom and vitality.
—JON KABAT-ZINN

Someone bumps into you on a crowded street; your teenager spills something on the rug; you realize you've missed an important appointment. What's your immediate thought? "Pay attention!" perhaps, or "Wake up!" From childhood we get—and give—the message that being conscious is the essence of living well, yet most of the time we walk around in a daze. How can we become more aware?

Mindfulness—being alert in every moment, open to the fullness of experience, and awake to who you really are—is a mark of enlightenment. Mindfulness meditation refers to specific practices that bring us into the present and teach us mental mastery. The Vietnamese Zen master Thich Nhat Hanh calls mindfulness both "a means and an end, the seed and the fruit." In *The Miracle of Mindfulness* he explains:

> *When we practice mindfulness in order to build up concentration, mindfulness is a seed. But mindfulness itself is the life of awareness: the presence of mindfulness means the presence of life, and therefore mindfulness is also the fruit. Mindfulness frees us of forgetfulness and dispersion and makes it possible to live fully every minute of life.*

All meditation is, in effect, concentration practice, since a certain degree of steadfast attention is required for even the most unstructured exercise. "In its most general sense meditation consists of thinking in a controlled manner," Rabbi Aryeh Kaplan explains in *Jewish Meditation*. "It is deciding exactly how one wishes to direct the mind for a period of time, and then doing it."

Focusing on how the mind works is central to Buddhism, and mindfulness is the seventh step in the Buddha's eightfold path to awakening. (The word *buddha* means "awake" in Pali, the language the Buddha spoke.) In the *Satipatthana Sutta*, the *Sutta on the Four Foundations of Mindfulness*, the Buddha taught that living mindfully means to maintain awareness of our bodies, our emotions, our thoughts, and the "objects of mind"—our experiences.

But you don't have to be a Buddhist—or even spiritually inclined—to benefit from this core teaching. Researchers have demonstrated its usefulness in mind/body healing. Jon Kabat-Zinn, founder of the Stress Reduction Clinic at the University of Massachusetts, has had remarkable results in teaching mindfulness techniques to master chronic pain and handle life's pressures more effectively. Kabat-Zinn is often credited with introducing the concept of mindfulness to the mainstream.

Daily life provides plenty of opportunities to become more aware of both our inner life and our surroundings. "Like it or not, this moment is all we really have to work with," Kabat-Zinn points out in *Wherever You Go, There You Are*. But when we fall into daydreaming and automatic responses, we find ourselves anywhere but here. A classic example of mind-*less*-ness is forgetting where you put your house keys, or "coming to" behind the wheel of your car and realizing you've driven the past ten blocks—or ten miles—in a fog. But mindlessness comes in a thousand guises, from a furious outburst to a misspent paycheck to a misspent life. Failing to be mindful not only mires us in

Inspiration: The Noble Eightfold Path

The Buddha taught that the end of suffering lies in neither self-gratification nor extreme asceticism but the Middle Way. This is the way of balance, integrating wisdom and compassion, mind and heart. The Buddha's message was that each of us can, in this lifetime, realize our inner perfection by following the eightfold path.

+ *Right view:* Seeing reality—the world and ourselves—clearly.

+ *Right intention:* Determining to be totally honest with ourselves and compassionate toward all beings.

+ *Right speech:* Telling the truth and refraining from gossip or unkind words.

+ *Right action:* Doing good and agreeing not to kill, steal, misuse sexual energy, or otherwise hurt others or ourselves.

+ *Right livelihood:* Making sure that our work serves others and ourselves, and does no harm.

+ *Right effort:* Giving up negative habits and behaviors and developing positive thoughts and actions.

+ *Right mindfulness:* Training ourselves to be aware and to live in the present.

+ *Right concentration:* Developing and maintaining a meditation practice.

unpleasant emotions like anger and fear but also removes us from whatever is happening in the present. We end up dwelling on past hurts and disappointments, or anticipating more problems in the future, and neglecting the needs or pleasures that are right in front of us.

Mindfulness practice helps us gather the scattered bits of our attention and refocus our awareness, so that we feel whole and alert. It pulls us into the moment, allowing us to be present for whatever is unfolding here and now. As our awareness deepens, we begin to gain more clarity—insight into the true nature of the mind, our own minds. If we are fully present in each moment of our lives, we will never have to look back in regret at how little we have truly experienced.

Being Here Now

The purpose of mindfulness training is summed up in the famous 1970s mantra, *Be Here Now*—the title of a popular book on meditation written by the popular spiritual teacher, Ram Dass. A former Harvard psychology professor named Richard Alpert, Ram Dass helped popularize meditation in America after visiting India in the late sixties and early seventies to study with his guru, Neem Karoli Baba.

The best examples of mindfulness in action are master teachers like the Dalai Lama and Thich Nhat Hanh. The word that comes to mind is *appropriate*. Their actions always seem to be clear, compassionate, and consonant with the needs of the moment. In *Awakening to the Buddha Within* the American Buddhist teacher Lama Surya Das tells a story about accompanying the Dalai Lama to dinner with another, much older lama, Pawo Rinpoche. The elderly man, whose eyesight was failing and who could no longer walk, suddenly stopped in midconversation and asked the Dalai Lama to rescue a tiny ant that was making its way across the floor in front of them. His Holiness got up and, with a smile, carefully deposited the insect outdoors. Later the Dalai Lama recounted this vignette as an example of Pawo Rinpoche's mindfulness: although nearly blind, he was fully aware of even the smallest creature and concerned for its well-being.

Most of us will probably never reach that level of sensitivity, but increased awareness is an attainable goal. There are ways to train the mind that anyone can use. Thich Nhat Hanh has devised a number of exercises to bring awareness to whatever situation is at hand (see pages 74–75 for examples). Some of the verses, such as "Entering the Meditation Room" and "Hearing the Bell," apply specifically to the meditation period; others, including "Driving the Car" and "Turning on the Light," can help us pay more attention to everyday life.

It's easy to argue that slowing down and scrutinizing every detail of life is impractical. If you spent the whole day doing that, how would you ever accomplish everything you need to do? But what if we told you that in the long run mindfulness will make your life run smoother and that you'll actually get more done? As you practice being aware in every situation, not just while sitting on your meditation cushion, your ability to respond appropriately and quickly to life's challenges will increase, and you will feel less rattled when events don't go according to plan. "I've got a short fuse," a newspaper editor admits, "but the closer I get to a deadline, ironically, the calmer I get. My years of meditation practice kick in, and I become very focused, so I can eliminate the extraneous, roll with whatever happens in each moment, and still get the copy in on time."

Cultivating Awareness

Vipassana—Pali for "insight," or "clear awareness"—is the oldest form of Buddhist meditation. Still widely practiced throughout Southern Asia, *Vipassana*, also known as Insight meditation, is one of the fastest-growing meditation practices in the United States. Insight meditation has put down roots here in part through a group of Americans who studied in Asia in the late sixties and seventies, then came back and established meditation centers. Among the best known of these teachers are Joseph Goldstein and Sharon Salzberg, cofounders of the Insight Meditation Society and the Barre Center for Buddhist Studies in Barre, Massachusetts; Jack Kornfield, founder of Spirit Rock Meditation Center in Woodacre, California; and Jon Kabat-Zinn.

Insight meditation can be practiced by anyone, regardless of spiritual belief. The

Try This: Mindfulness Verses

ENTERING THE MEDITATION ROOM

Entering the meditation room,
I see my true mind.
I vow that once I sit down,
all disturbances will stop.

HEARING THE BELL

Listen, listen,
this wonderful sound
brings me back to my true self.

SITTING DOWN

Sitting here
is like sitting under the Bodhi tree.
My body is mindfulness itself,
entirely free from distraction.

ADJUSTING MEDITATION POSTURE

Feelings come and go
like clouds in a windy sky.
Conscious breathing
is my anchor.

SERVING FOOD

In this food
I see clearly the presence
of the entire universe
supporting my existence.

DRINKING TEA

This cup of tea in my two hands,
mindfulness is held uprightly!
My mind and body dwell
in the very here and now.

USING THE TELEPHONE

Words can travel thousands of miles.
May my words create mutual understanding and love.
May they be as beautiful as gems,
as lovely as flowers.

DRIVING THE CAR

Before starting the car,
I know where I am going.
The car and I are one.
If the car goes fast, I go fast.

TURNING ON THE WATER

Water flows from high in the mountains.
Water runs deep in the Earth.
Miraculously, water comes to us,
and sustains all life.

TURNING ON THE LIGHT

Forgetfulness is the darkness;
mindfulness is the light.
I bring awareness
to shine upon all life.

—THICH NHAT HANH, *PRESENT MOMENT, WONDERFUL MOMENT*

purpose is straightforward: to explore—and gradually free ourselves from—the habits, beliefs, and prejudices that limit our perspective and separate us from our deepest selves and our fellow beings. It's often said that cultivating mindfulness is like shining a light into a dark corner: the result is the ability to see reality clearly.

The essence of Insight practice is "bare attention"—opening your awareness to whatever is happening from moment to moment. Compared to concentration practices in which the mind is focused on a single object, Insight meditation is more open ended and inclusive. "Our bodies, minds, feelings, mental states, perceptions, sounds, and sight are all equally embraced in the clear, sensitive light of mindfulness without preference or distinction," explains Christina Feldman, cofounder of Gaia House meditation center in Devon, England, in *Principles of Meditation.* By paying attention to both our inner and outer experience, we gradually deepen our understanding of ourselves and the world, and come to know the truth underlying all.

How do you practice mindfulness? One way is simply to follow the breath (see Chapter 4: "Finding Stillness"). Later, to strengthen your awareness, you can move on to "noting" (See "Mental Noting," page 77). In noting practice you observe your experience with an attentive but relaxed mind. As sensations arise, you do not try to change them; rather, you label them. If, for example, you become aware of a sound, you might silently repeat, *Hearing, hearing.* Similarly, you would note smelling, or sensations such as cold or heat, as you perceive them. Even pain can be an object of noting. What is its exact nature: Is it burning? Pulling? Tingling? All sensations are constantly changing; noting practice helps us acknowledge the transience of our experience.

You can continue noting when you shift to walking meditation (see Chapter 9: "Moving with Spirit"), or even to everyday activities, such as eating. You might, for example, repeat, *Intending, intending,* as you prepare to lift your foot or your fork, then note each aspect of the activity: raising the foot or lifting the arm; placing the foot on the ground or the food in your mouth; feeling the ground or tasting your food. As you continue practicing mindfulness, you will eventually become aware of consciousness itself—the workings of your mind, quite apart from the content. At that stage you would simply note, *Knowing.*

Ultimately, what Insight meditation shows us is that we are the prisoners of our *thoughts* about our experience: we are identified with our opinions, our "stories" about

Try This: Mental Noting

The art of mental noting, as a tool of meditation, requires practice and experimentation. Labeling objects of experience as they arise supports mindfulness in many different ways.

Noting should be done very softly, like a whisper in the mind, but with enough precision and accuracy so that it connects directly with the object. For example, you might label each breath, silently saying *In, out* or *Rising, falling.* In addition you may also note every other appearance that arises in meditation. When thoughts arise, note thinking. If physical sensations become predominant, note pressure, vibration, tension, tingling, or whatever it might be. If sounds or images come into the foreground, note hearing or seeing.

The note itself can be seen as another appearance in the mind, even as it functions to keep us undistracted. Labeling, like putting a frame around a picture, helps you recognize the object more clearly and gives greater focus and precision to your observation.

Mental noting supports mindfulness in another way, by showing us when awareness is reactive and when it is truly mindful. For example, we may be aware of pain in the body but through a filter of aversion. . . . You sit and note, *Pain, pain,* but perhaps with a gritted-teeth tone to the note; the tone makes obvious the actual state of mind. Quite amazingly, simply changing the tone of the note can often change your mind state.

—JOSEPH GOLDSTEIN, *INSIGHT MEDITATION*

what reality is. "It is important to make thoughts the object of mindfulness," emphasizes Joseph Goldstein in *The Experience of Insight.* When you watch the play of thoughts in your mind, you eventually come to realize their ephemeral nature and become less reactive to them.

Why is it so hard for us to see reality as it is? In *A Path with Heart* Jack Kornfield sheds light on the matter:

The unawakened mind tends to make war against the way things are. . . . [And] contemporary society fosters our mental tendency to deny or suppress our awareness of reality. Ours is a society of denial that conditions us to protect ourselves from any direct difficulty or discomfort.

We expend enormous energy denying our insecurity, fighting pain, death, and loss, and hiding from the basic truths of the natural world and of our own nature. . . . To stop the war we need to begin with ourselves.

Mindfulness practice gives us a way to experience—and penetrate—our own denial.

Opening the Wisdom Eye

If the essence of Insight meditation is bare attention, the focus of *zazen*, or Zen practice, is a kind of stop-time in which we experience pure being. As the scholar D. T. Suzuki explains in *An Introduction to Zen Buddhism*, "The discipline of Zen consists in opening the mental eye in order to look into the very reason of existence."

Zen is often called "direct transmission outside the sutras," because awareness comes not from sermons or texts but from spontaneous, personal experience of the truth—"getting it," in other words. Zen is said to have originated when the Buddha responded to a question about the meaning of life by simply holding up a flower; only one student in the crowd understood. Most Zen practitioners spend many years in meditation before that moment of awareness occurs. But it is the profound simplicity of Zen practice and its emphasis on direct experiencing of the truth that accounts for its enduring appeal among Westerners.

Inspiration: What Is Zen?

Zen is not a puzzle; it cannot be solved by wit. It is a spiritual food for those who want to learn what life is and what our mission is in this world. Mere scholarly pursuits will never lead to realization. Zen is not so much a religion as it is the essence of life itself, the naked truth of the universe, which is none other than the experience of Mind.

—NYOGEN SENZAKI, FROM *NAMU DAI BOSA*
BY NYOGEN SENZAKI, SOEN NAKAGAWA, AND EIDO SHIMANO

Zen migrated to China from India in the sixth century, then to Japan in the twelfth century; it also spread to Korea and Vietnam. (The Chinese name, Ch'an, and Zen both come from *dhyana*, Sanskrit for "meditation.") Americans first encountered Zen early in the twentieth century, as a handful of Japanese masters began coming to the United States to teach. By the 1950s Zen was popular in intellectual circles, thanks to Beat-generation writers such as Jack Kerouac and Allen Ginsberg, and the philosopher Alan Watts, who wrote widely and influentially on the subject. Over the next two decades, as Zen practice increased, books on the teachings of modern Zen masters became instant classics. Among the best known are *The Three Pillars of Zen*—introductory lectures by Hakuin Yasutani Roshi (*roshi* is Japanese for "venerable teacher"), edited by the American roshi Philip Kapleau—and *Zen Mind, Beginner's Mind*, talks by Shunryu Suzuki Roshi, the founder of the San Francisco Zen Center.

Zen in America fanned out in a range of approaches, from the formal monastic tradition of Japanese *roshis* such as Joshu Sasaki and Eido Shimano, to the more eclectic practices of Suzuki Roshi, Taizen Maezumi Roshi, and the Korean master Seung Sahn, to the homegrown paths of American teachers such as Robert Aitken Roshi, Bernard Glassman Roshi, Charlotte Joko Beck, Joan Halifax Roshi, and Toni Packer. Regardless of style, in substance all Zen practice promotes mindfulness. As Kapleau Roshi explains in *Awakening to Zen*, "The aim of Zen training is awakening, and the living of a life that is creative, harmonious, and *alive*."

You will sometimes hear people speak of Zen practice as "sitting down in the heart of the problem" (see "Sanzen Is Zazen," page 80). Zazen erodes the false ego barrier that separates us from others and from insight into our own true nature. When for an instant "I" and "other" disappear, we experience only the sense of being one with all creation. Zazen, it is sometimes said, "uses the mind to go through the mind—or lose the mind." With continued practice the mind becomes, as Kapleau Roshi puts it, "like a silent missile, to penetrate the barrier of the five senses and the discursive intellect."

Zen masters in America are notoriously coy about describing enlightenment experiences. In Zen's characteristically paradoxical logic ("crazy wisdom") each person's moment of realization is seen as unique, momentous—and at the same time, no big deal. *Three Pillars of Zen* is unusual among Zen books in that it relates a number of these experiences. In one instance a student reports, "I've totally disappeared. Buddha is!" The difficulty of trying to explain this state of oneness is that as soon as you shift from experiencing it to observing it, you have already moved back into ordinary dualistic awareness. Early masters famously conveyed the truth of Zen by a gesture: a raised finger, a slap, a shout.

Zazen can be practiced without a teacher: in its simplest form it merely involves sitting up straight and concentrating on the breath. For ongoing study a teacher is recommended: the private interview (*dokusan*) is the heart of this relationship, with one-on-one teaching that is more "show" than "tell." By tradition Zen masters test students' understanding in apparently nonsensical exchanges that nonetheless speak volumes. One woman recalls her teacher crouching in front of her and saying exuberantly, "Let's be frogs!" He rightly gauged that his playfulness would surprise her into profound awareness.

Zen practice commonly falls into one of two schools—Soto and Rinzai. Soto Zen is bare-bones Zen: the practice is *shikan-taza*, or "just sitting." But with nothing to attend to, the mind is quickly distracted. Rinzai Zen uses one-pointed focus—concentration on breath-counting or on a conundrum known as a *koan* (pronounced KOH-ahn)—to bring a student to realization. Koans like "What is the sound of one hand clapping?" and "Show me your original face, the one you had before your mother and father were born" are typically associated with Zen, but there are hundreds more in the traditional collections. There is no one "right" answer to a koan; the student must demonstrate his

Inspiration: Sanzen Is Zazen

When you sit down in zazen, you don't know why. If you think about it, you can come up with many reasons. But the reasons don't hit the mark exactly. . . . What you want is just to be present, right in the middle of true reality, where you and zazen exactly merge, nothing else. To sit zazen is to call upon something, and to sit zazen is exactly the something you are calling upon. You sit exactly in the middle of something you are always looking for and calling upon. We don't know what it is but it's always there. If you sit down, you feel something, you taste it. . . . Whoever we are, whatever reason we have to decide to sit down, immediately we can sit with our whole mind, our whole heart.

—DAININ KATAGIRI, *RETURNING TO SILENCE*

understanding to the master's satisfaction. And the solution is not an end in itself; the koan is merely a tool to spur the meditator to deep realization. Pondering it is more a matter of *absorbing* the koan than thinking about it. In a sense the process resembles the advice offered by Rainer Maria Rilke in *Letters to a Young Poet*:

> *. . . try to love the* questions themselves *like locked rooms and like books that are written in a very foreign tongue. Do not now seek the answers, which cannot be given you because you would not be able to live them. . . . Live the* questions *now. Perhaps you will then, gradually, without noticing it, live along some distant day into the answer.*

By "living the question"—keeping the koan alive in one's mind day and night—the meditator eventually reaches the "aha" moment of understanding.

Beginner's Mind, Open Mind

Koan study is the Zen way to squeeze the rational mind till it gives up its certainty and lets go of its preconceptions about reality. Zen teaches us about *unlearning*—stripping

Try This: Who Am I?

The question is designed to let you keep probing all the different concepts you have about yourself. You make a list. You might start with your name: "I'm Bernie." But then you might think, "I'm not just Bernie. I'm an engineer." Then again, "I'm a father," or "I'm a brother." And so on. But whoever you come up with is not who you are. It's one of the roles you play. But if you keep going, past all these roles and identities, you might eventually find yourself in a state of not knowing. . . . When we let go of all concepts and ideas, we experience ourselves as we really are. . . .

—BERNARD GLASSMAN AND RICK FIELDS, *INSTRUCTIONS TO THE COOK* away the barriers to clear awareness, rather than trying to learn more. There is a classic story about a professor who came to the great master Nan-in to find out about Zen. Nan-in poured him a cup of tea—and kept pouring, till tea spilled over the sides of the cup. Finally, the professor could stand it no longer and protested. Nan-in explained, "Like that cup your mind is overfull—full of your opinions and conceptions. How can I show you Zen until you empty your mind?"

The mind that is empty and receptive is known in Japanese as *shoshin*—"beginner's mind." (As Shunryu Suzuki famously put it, "In the beginner's mind there are many possibilities, but in the expert's there are few.") This is the starting point of the spiritual journey—when we begin to question our certainty about life, about ourselves. "Doubt," Bernard Glassman Roshi and Rick Fields tell us in *Instructions to the Cook*, "allows us to explore things in an open and fresh way." To begin this unraveling process Glassman suggests meditating on an age-old question and fundamental mystery: "Who am I?" (see page 81).

Zen practice turns up the heat. Here is where determination comes in. As anyone who has sat a seven-day Zen *sesshin* (meditation retreat) will attest, zazen is not for the fainthearted. Charlotte Joko Beck, teacher at the Zen Center in San Diego, writes in *Everyday Zen*, "A zendo is not a place for bliss and relaxation, but a furnace room for

Inspiration: Moment to Moment

There is a famous Zen story that illustrates mindfulness and the importance of living in the present, not the past or future.

Two monks were walking together in a rainstorm when they came upon a young woman in front of a puddle that was too deep for her to cross. One monk picked her up, carried her over the puddle, and set her down on the other side. The monks continued on their way, but at the end of the day the other monk blurted out, "How could you pick her up? You know monks aren't supposed to touch women!"

The first monk turned to his friend. "I put that woman down hours ago. Why are you still carrying her?"

—TRADITIONAL ZEN TALE

Inspiration: Waking Up

Intellectual questions elicit intellectual answers; they won't transform your life. Only when you are driven to cry from your guts, "I must, I *will* find out!" will your question be answered. And that will be your awakening, for in the profoundest sense the question and answer are not two; they only appear so because of your discriminating intellect, which divides what is essentially indivisible.

—PHILIP KAPLEAU ROSHI, *ZEN DAWN IN THE WEST*

the combustion of our egoistic delusions. What tools do we need to use? Only one. We've all heard of it, yet we use it very seldom. It's called *attention."*

Attention. Concentration. Mindfulness. This is the attitude we cultivate in meditation practice so that we can make it the foundation of our everyday lives.

RESOURCES

BOOKS

Aitken, Robert. *Original Dwelling Place.* Washington, DC: Counterpoint, 1996.

————. *Taking the Path of Zen.* San Francisco: North Point Press, 1982.

Beck, Charlotte Joko. *Everyday Zen.* San Francisco: Harper San Francisco, 1989.

Bhikku, Buddhadasa. *Mindfulness with Breathing.* Somerville, Mass.: Wisdom, 1996.

Boorstein, Sylvia. *Don't Just Do Something, Sit There.* San Francisco: Harper San Francisco, 1996.

Das, Lama Surya. *Awakening to the Buddha Within.* New York: Broadway, 1999.

Dass, Ram. *Be Here Now.* New York: Crown, 1971.

Feldman, Christina. *Principles of Meditation.* London, England: Thorsons, 1998.

Flickstein, Matthew. *Journey to the Center: A Meditation Workbook.* Somerville, Mass.: Wisdom, 1998.

Glassman, Bernard, and Rick Fields. *Instructions to the Cook.* New York: Bell Tower, 1996.

Goldstein, Joseph. *The Experience of Insight.* Boston: Shambhala, 1983.

———. *Insight Meditation.* Boston: Shambhala, 1994.

Goldstein, Joseph, and Jack Kornfield. *Seeking the Heart of Wisdom.* Boston: Shambhala, 1987.

Goleman, Daniel, and Ram Dass. *The Meditative Mind: Varieties of Meditative Experience.* New York: Jeremy P. Tarcher/Putnam, 1988.

Gunaratana, Ven. Henepola. *Mindfulness in Plain English.* Somerville, Mass.: Wisdom, 1991.

Kabat-Zinn, Jon. *Wherever You Go, There You Are.* New York: Hyperion, 1994.

Kaplan, Aryeh. *Jewish Meditation.* New York: Schocken, 1985.

Kapleau, Philip, Roshi. *Awakening to Zen.* New York: Scribner, 1997.

———. *Zen: Dawn in the West.* New York: Doubleday, 1979.

Kapleau, Philip, ed. *The Three Pillars of Zen.* Boston: Beacon, 1965.

Katagiri, Dainin. *Returning to Silence.* Boston: Shambhala, 1988.

Kerouac, Jack. *Dharma Bums.* New York: Penguin, 1991.

Kornfield, Jack. *A Path with Heart.* New York: Bantam, 1993.

Levine, Stephen. *A Gradual Awakening.* New York: Anchor, 1989.

Nhat Hahn, Thich. *Breathe! You Are Alive: Sutra on the Full Awareness of Breathing.* Berkeley: Parallax Press, 1996.

———. *The Miracle of Mindfulness.* Boston: Beacon Press, 1976.

———. *Peace Is Every Step.* Arnold Kotler, ed. New York: Bantam, 1992.

———. *Present Moment, Wonderful Moment.* Berkeley: Parallax Press, 1990.

———. *Zen Keys.* New York: Doubleday, 1994.

Reps, Paul. *Zen Flesh, Zen Bones.* Boston: Tuttle, 1998.

Rilke, Rainer Maria. *Letters to a Young Poet.* New York: Norton, 1934.

Rosenberg, Larry. *Breath by Breath: The Liberating Practice of Insight Meditation.* Boston: Shambhala, 1998.

Senzaki, Nyogen, Soen Nakagawa, and Eido Shimano. *Namu Dai Bosa.* New York: Theatre Arts Books, 1976.

Smith, Jean, ed. *Breath Sweeps Mind: A First Guide to Meditation Practice.* New York: Riverhead, 1998.

Suzuki, D. T. *An Introduction to Zen Buddhism.* New York: Grove Press, 1964.

Suzuki Roshi, Shunryu. *Zen Mind, Beginner's Mind.* New York: Weatherhill, 1970.

Watts, Alan. *Essential Alan Watts.* Berkeley: Celestial Arts, 1977.

————. *The Way of Zen.* New York: Vintage, 1999.

PERIODICALS

Inquiring Mind: A Journal of the Vipassana Community
PO Box 9999, North Berkeley Station
Berkeley, CA 94709
biannual

Mindfulness Bell
Community of Mindful Living
PO Box 7355
Berkeley, CA 94707
(510) 527–3751
three times a year

Shambhala Sun
1585 Barrington Street, Suite 300
Halifax, Nova Scotia
Canada B3J IZ8
(902) 422–8404
www.shambhala.com
bimonthly; Buddhism, culture, meditation, life

Tricycle: The Buddhist Review
92 Vandam Street
New York, NY 10013
(212) 645–1143
www.tricycle.com
quarterly

AUDIO/VIDEO

Break Through Difficult Emotions. Shinzen Young. How to use mindfulness meditation to transform painful feelings (Sounds True).

Five Classic Meditations. Shinzen Young. Practical guide to mantra, *Vipassana* (Insight) meditation, Karma yoga, lovingkindness practice, and Kabbalah meditation (Audio Renaissance).

The Inner Art of Meditation. Jack Kornfield. Mindfulness meditation for beginners, from the founder of Spirit Rock Meditation Center (Sounds True).

Insight Meditation: An In-depth Correspondence Course. Sharon Salzberg and Joseph Goldstein. Twelve-month meditation course taught by the Insight Meditation Center cofounders via cassettes and e-mail (Sounds True).

Meditation for Beginners. Jack Kornfield. Mindfulness meditation in four basic steps (Sounds True).

Mindful Living. Thich Nhat Hanh. Teachings on love, mindfulness, and meditation by a well-known Vietnamese Zen Buddhist master (Sounds True).

Natural Perfection. Lama Surya Das. Teachings, meditations, and chants in the Dzogchen tradition of Tibet (Sounds True).

A Path with Heart. Jack Kornfield. A definitive guide to *Vipassana* (Insight) meditation (Sounds True).

Pebbles and Pearls. Jon Kabat-Zinn. Mindfulness practice for daily life, taught by the founder and former director of the Stress Reduction Clinic at the UMass Medical Center (Sounds True).

Plum Village Meditations. Thich Nhat Hahn and Sister Jina van Hengel. Guided meditations and bell-ringing from the celebrated Zen center (Sounds True).

The Present Moment. Thich Nhat Hahn. A retreat on the practice of mindfulness, led by a modern Zen master (Sounds True).

Relaxation & Mindfulness. Daniel Goleman with Tara Bennett-Goleman and Mark Epstein, M.D. Daily antistress meditations from the author of *Emotional Intelligence* (Sound Horizons).

The Science of Enlightenment. Shinzen Young. Awakening through self-investigation (Sounds True).

Taming the Mind. Sogyal Rinpoche. Practicing mindfulness for calm in everyday life, from the author of *The Tibetan Book of Living and Dying* (New Dimensions).

Your Buddha Nature. Jack Kornfield. Teachings on Buddhism's foundation for mindful living, the Ten Perfections (Sounds True).

ORGANIZATIONS

Barre Center for Buddhist Studies
149 Lockwood Rd.
PO Box 7
Barre, MA 10005
(978) 355–2347

Cambridge Insight Meditation Center
331 Broadway
Cambridge, MA 02139
(617) 441–9038

Cambridge Zen Center
199 Auburn Street
Cambridge, MA 02139
(617) 576–3229

Center for Mindfulness, Stress Reduction Clinic
UMass Medical Center
419 Belmont Ave. 2nd floor
Worcester, MA 01604

Dharma Seed Tape Library
Box 66
Wendell Depot, MA 01380

Dzogchen Foundation
PO Box 734
Cambridge, MA 02140
(617) 628–1702

Gaia House
West Ogwell, Newton Abbot,
Devon TQ12 6EN, England
(011) 441–626–333613

Green Gulch Farm Zen Center
1601 Shoreline Highway
Sausalito, CA 94965
(415) 383–3134

Insight Meditation Society
1230 Pleasant Street
Barre, MA 01005
(978) 355–4378

Mindfulness Practice
PO Box 548
Quechee, VT 05059
(802) 280–9903

Plum Village, Meyrac
Loubes-Bernac
47120 France
(011) 33–553–947540
lh office@plumvillage.org

San Francisco Zen Center
300 Page Street
San Francisco, CA 94102
(415) 863–3136

Spirit Rock Center
PO Box 909-B
Woodacre, CA 94973
(415) 488–0164

Tassajara Zen Mountain Center
39171 Tassajara Road
Carmel Valley, CA 93924
(831) 659–2229
mailing address:
c/o SF Zen Center
300 Page Street
San Francisco, CA 94102

Upaya Foundation
1404 Cerro Gordo Road
Santa Fe, NM 87501
(505) 986–8518

Vipassana Support Institute
4070 Albright Avenue
Los Angeles, CA 90066
(310) 915–1943

Zen Center of Los Angeles
923 South Normandie Avenue
Los Angeles, CA 90006
(213) 387–2351

Zen Mountain Monastery
Box 197, South Plank Road
Mt. Tremper, NY 12457
(914) 688–2228

Zen Studies Society
223 East 67th Street
New York, NY 10021
(212) 861–3333

WEB SITES

www.dharma.org
Homepage of the Insight Meditation Society in Barre, Massachusetts, offering interviews with well-known Buddhist teachers, *Insight* magazine on-line, and more.

www.dzogchen.org/foundation/about/html
Site of the Dzogchen Foundation, set up to preserve and transmit Tibetan Dzogchen teachings to Westerners.

www.mindfulnesstapes.com
Jon Kabat-Zinn's Web site, to order tapes on mindfulness and find out about the author.

www.PeacemakerCommunity.org/upaya
Information on Buddhist study and retreat center founded by Joan Halifax Roshi of the Zen Peacemaker Order.

www.sfzc.com
Maintained by San Francisco Zen Center, one of the oldest Zen communities in the United States, and its affiliated Green Gulch Farm and Tassajara Mountain Monastery.

www.zencenter.org
Information on activities at the city and mountain communities of the Zen Center of Los Angeles.

www.zenstudies.org
Maintained by the Zen Studies Society of New York City and its affiliated monastery, International Dai Bosatsu Zendo.

Heart-Centering

6

My religion is kindness.
—HIS HOLINESS THE DALAI LAMA

Every day, we can open a newspaper or watch the news on TV and see signs of a world in distress. And we have only to spend a few hours alone with ourselves to get in touch with the distress we carry inside. At any given moment, most of us are dealing with some sort of discomfort or disappointment: the failure to get something or someone we wanted; the loss of someone or something dear; a health crisis, or an ego blow, or any of a thousand setbacks affecting ourselves and those close to us. Even if all is well in our world, our inner voices are constantly firing instructions and recriminations: *Stand up straight. Don't talk so much. Hurry up. Why didn't you . . . ?*

Great spiritual teachers of past and present, such as Jesus, the Dalai Lama, and Mother Teresa inspire us with their compassion in the face of turmoil and suffering. They are examples of how to be loving and forgiving toward all beings, including ourselves. "Do unto others as you would have them do unto you" and "Love thy neighbor as thyself" were Christ's messages to his followers. And the Dalai Lama has said, "My message is the practice of compassion, love, and kindness. Whether one believes in a religion or not, and whether one believes in rebirth or not, there isn't anyone who doesn't appreciate compassion, mercy." Mother Teresa, when asked what the purpose of life was, responded simply: "To give and receive love."

The Vietnamese Zen master Thich Nhat Hanh calls compassion a verb, to emphasize that it is not a concept but an *activity*—a way of being in the world that brings peace to oneself as well as to others. As a dynamic force compassion is both a motivation behind spiritual practice and also a result of practice. For those whose deepest yearning is to relieve suffering—their own, others', the world's—heart-centered practices offer a sympathetic path.

Two of the most effective heart-centered practices—*metta* (Pali for "lovingkindness") and *tonglen* (Tibetan for "giving and receiving")—are Buddhist in origin but draw on universal principles. Anyone would find them helpful to melt the heart and awaken caring. (In one of the exercises in this chapter, "Giving and Taking," on page 100, *tonglen* practice is given a Christian focus.) Central to the practice of compassion is forgiveness, which opens us to the divine in one another—the first step toward healing ourselves and society.

Awakening the Heart

"True love has the power to heal and transform the situation around us and bring a deep meaning to our lives," writes Thich Nhat Hanh in *Teachings on Love.* He does not, of course, mean romantic love, but *metta*—*maitri* in Sanskrit—a nonjudging, nongrasping kind of caring and attention.

The Buddha gave a number of teachings on love. The *Metta Sutta*—*Discourse on Love*—is one of his most famous. As the story goes, the Buddha sent some monks into the forest to meditate. They ran back to him complaining that tree spirits were terrorizing them and asked permission to meditate elsewhere. The Buddha offered them something better: he instructed them in *metta* practice to transmute fear (see page 94).

Metta, also known as lovingkindness, is said to have been so effective that the loving energy generated by the monks transformed the tree spirits into allies.

One of the foremost American teachers of lovingkindness is Sharon Salzberg. The word *metta* is inscribed in big letters above the entrance to the Insight Meditation Center in Barre, Massachusetts, which she cofounded. According to the Buddha's teachings *metta* is the first of the four *brahma-viharas*—qualities or states of consciousness to which we aspire. (The others are compassion, or *karuna*; sympathetic joy, *mudita*; and equanimity, *upekkha*.) As Salzberg points out, the Buddha encouraged us to let go of "unskillful" habits and mental states that cause us pain, such as anger and fear, and to cultivate the capacity for love and happiness.

Metta is a subtle, complex, and powerful practice. Even a basic understanding of it can open the way to better relations with ourselves and others. With diligent effort barriers of hurt and anger and separation that seem impenetrable will begin to fall away. "The word *metta* in Pali actually means 'friendship,' " notes Sharon Salzberg. "So it's the art of developing friendship with yourself and with all of life." *Metta* is a quality of compassion that views *what is*—whatever that is—without hatred or rejection. It leads you to accept all aspects of yourself, even those you find loathsome.

We all want to feel good about ourselves and loving toward other people. But despite our intentions, much of the time we end up feeling closed off and unloving. An important aspect of lovingkindness is the recognition that we are all bound together in a web of interconnectedness. "No one is separate, however separate we might feel," Sharon Salzberg points out.

We connect with each other through our desire to be happy—a desire that all beings share. The Dalai Lama is often quoted as saying that the purpose of life is to be happy and to make others happy. As Sharon Salzberg writes in *Lovingkindness*, "The spirit of *metta* is unconditional: open, and unobstructed."

Practicing Lovingkindness

How do we practice *metta*? Sitting in meditation, we construct a series of phrases that express what we wish for ourself and, ultimately, for all beings. The traditional phrases are *May I be free from danger, May I have mental happiness, May I have physical happiness, May I have ease of well-being.* Sharon Salzberg suggests ways to tailor the wording to your own needs (see "Metta or Lovingkindness Practice," page 94).

The customary progression is to move from having *metta* for yourself, to a "bene-

Try This: Metta or Lovingkindness Practice

In doing *metta* practice we gently repeat phrases that express what we wish, first for our-selves and then for others. These aspirations should be deeply felt and enduring (not some-thing like "May I find a good show on television tonight"). Classically, four phrases are used. You can experiment with them, alter them, or simply choose an alternative set.

May I be free from danger, or *May I be free from fear.* We ultimately wish that all be-ings as well as ourselves have a sense of safety, have freedom from internal torment and external violence.

May I have mental happiness, or *May I be happy.* If we were in touch with our own love-liness, if we felt less fearful of others, if we trusted our ability to love, we would have men-tal happiness. In the same vein, if we could relate skillfully to the torments of the mind that arise, we would have mental happiness.

May I have physical happiness, or *May I be healthy.* With this phrase we wish ourselves the enjoyment of health, freedom from physical pain, and harmony with our bodies.

May I have ease of well-being, or *May I dwell in peace.* We wish that the elements of our daily life, such as relationships, family issues, and livelihood, be accomplished grace-fully and easily.

Sit comfortably. You can start with half an hour of daily practice. Begin with five minutes of reflection on the good within you or your wish to be happy. Then choose the phrases that express what you most deeply wish for yourself, and repeat them silently over and over again. Develop a relaxed pace; there is no need to rush. If your attention wanders, or if diffi-cult feelings or memories arise, try to let go of them in the spirit of kindness and begin again.

After about ten minutes, change the subject from yourself to a benefactor—someone you deeply love or are grateful to or inspired by. Then, repeat the practice, substituting the name of a neutral person, someone you neither like nor dislike. Next, repeat the phrases fo-cusing on a difficult person—someone with whom you experience conflict, fear, or anger. It is best not to begin with the person who has harmed you most but gradually to work up to those with whom you have the most difficulty. (As an alternative to choosing a difficult per-son, you can experiment with directing *metta* toward a difficult aspect of yourself. You can factor" (someone you are grateful to or inspired by), then a friend, then a neutral person (someone toward whom you don't have strong feelings), then an enemy, or difficult person. In meditating on these phrases, *metta* practice is like any concentration practice, Sharon Salzberg says: "Your attention will constantly wander, and you will have to begin again without feeling discouraged."

What is important about *metta* practice, Salzberg explains, "is that it harnesses the power of intention. Every time we say one of those phrases, it's like planting a seed in the ground. Not all seeds flower right away, so you may not feel love right away. But it's important not to feel badly about that. You often see the fruits of this practice more in your daily life than when you're sitting on your meditation cushion."

As we begin to see the goodness in others, we start to feel a connection to them. Letting go of defensiveness and adversarial attitudes opens us to the possibility of caring. *Metta* opens the door to true intimacy.

If you have reservations about practicing *metta,* you can explore this principle in an exercise devised by a popular Jesuit retreat leader, the late Anthony de Mello. Called "Finding God in All Things," (see page 96), it invites you to focus on a favorite object and discover what it can teach you about seeing the goodness in yourself and others.

Forgiveness

What if a person has hurt you deeply or caused serious harm? How can you just forget all that and embrace someone you hate? Forgiving does not necessarily mean forgetting, Sharon Salzberg points out. "Having *metta* for a person does not mean giving up your sense of self-protection."

If the wrong is grievous—physical or emotional abuse, say, or abandonment—forgiveness may be a long and arduous journey. When you first start sending *metta* to a difficult person, don't pick history's worst villain or the person who has hurt you the most, Salzberg suggests. "Start with someone you find a little bit disagreeable, then slowly build to the harder ones. What you're building is your confidence in your own ability to love."

Ultimately, having *metta* for someone means more than recognizing the connection between you and the other person. "It also means realizing the pain of your own anger," Sharon Salzberg notes. "If we're living in a web of vengefulness, we're defined by that."

Try This: Finding God in All Things

Choose some object that you use frequently: a pen, a cup. It should be an object that you can easily hold in your hands. Let the object rest on the palms of your outstretched hands. Now close your eyes and get the feel of it. Become as fully aware of it as possible.

Now explore the object with your fingers or both your hands. It is important that you do this gently and reverently. Explore its roughness or smoothness, its hardness or softness, its warmth or coldness.

Now become acquainted with your object through your sense of sight. Open your eyes and see every possible detail in it.

Now place the object in front of you and speak to it. Begin by asking questions about its life, its origin, its future. Listen while it unfolds to you the secret of its being and its destiny.

Your object has some hidden wisdom to reveal to you about yourself. What is it? What does it want from you?

Now imagine that you and this object are in the presence of Jesus Christ. Listen to what he has to say to you and the object. What do the two of you say in response?

Now look at your object once more. Has your attitude toward it changed? Is there any change in your attitude toward the other objects around you?

—ADAPTED FROM *SADHANA: A WAY TO GOD* BY ANTHONY DE MELLO

Forgiveness is a core teaching of nearly every path. Forgiving others is as practical as it is spiritual, bringing not only immediate relief but also long-term peace of mind. Jesus encouraged us to "turn the other cheek" not from cowardice or charity but from recognition of the power of vengeance to destroy the one who bears the grudge. Alcoholics Anonymous calls even righteous anger "a dubious luxury" that can lead the resentful person back to drinking. And the Buddha compared anger to a hot coal: when you pick it up to fire it at the enemy, it burns your own hand first. As the Dalai Lama observes, "With anger, hatred, it is very difficult to feel inner peace. In every major world religion the emphasis is on brotherhood."

Ill will toward others is often a projection of our own internal state of self-hatred or low self-esteem. Anger eats away at health and well-being. When psychologist Joan Borysenko was doing mind-body research at Harvard Medical School, she found that holding on to resentments was the leading cause of stress and that forgiveness was the most effective means of breaking free.

Self-forgiveness is the first step. Forgiveness "has nothing to do with condoning poor behavior in ourselves and others," Borysenko states in *The Ways of the Mystic*. "Rather, it calls us to responsibility. In forgiving ourselves we make the journey from guilt for what we have done (or not done) to celebration of what we have become." (See "Practice Self-Forgiveness," below.)

Mistakes are a sacred opportunity to reconsider our own ill-conceived behavior,

Try This: Practice Self-Forgiveness

Before sleep, review your day, beginning with evening and working back toward morning. Did you do, think, or say anything for which you feel regret? If so, think about what contributed to the situation(s) and whether anything needs to be put right. Do you need to make amends to someone or make some change in your life? Commit to taking any necessary actions, and give thanks for what you have learned. Then ask God to forgive you, as you have forgiven yourself.

—JOAN BORYSENKO, PHD, *THE WAYS OF THE MYSTIC*

make amends to ourselves and others, and begin anew. *Repentance* literally means "to rethink," Borysenko notes. Willingness to forgive opens us to God's grace.

Teshuvah—the Jewish practice of repentance—focuses on eliciting God's forgiveness. *Teshuvah* can be outer directed, as in performing specific acts of compassion or respect to others, or it can be inner directed, as in reflecting deeply on harm you have done. Such practices not only earn us God's forgiveness but also help assuage the accumulated guilt of humankind. As Rabbi David Cooper explains in *Silence, Simplicity, and Solitude,* "[The] process of identification, regret, and positive assertion provides a method of working to repair the spiritual parts that are broken in us and in the world."

Heart-centered practices can help us work through anger, remorse, and guilt, reconnect with the Divine, and recognize our interconnectedness. We can't necessarily change others, but we can change our own feelings and behavior toward them (see "Six Steps to Forgiveness," below). The Hindu greeting *Namaste* means "The divine in me bows to the divine in you." In the ritual of bowing we honor the essential godliness of one another. Joan Borysenko recommends making respectful acknowledgment of oth-

Try This: Six Steps to Forgiveness

1. Think of a person or situation about which you feel anger or anguish or bitterness or regret. Hold that image like a prism to the light, examining it from every angle.
2. Focus on your role in the painful relationship or situation: where were you wrong or thoughtless or mistaken?
3. Imagine how you would feel if you were no longer angry or upset at the person or situation.
4. Explore the possibility of making amends, whether that means an apology, repayment of a debt, or some other form of restitution—or simply being willing to let go of your resentment.
5. Make the amend—unless it would harm someone.
6. Make a commitment not to harbor resentments in the future.

ers a daily practice. Whenever you see someone, silently say *"Namaste"* or something from your own spiritual tradition; Borysenko uses *"Shalom"* or "Peace be with you."

Practicing Compassion

Sometimes the world's suffering seems overwhelming. We may turn away from it out of sadness or frustration that there isn't more we can do to change it. However, spiritual teachers point out that daily life offers plenty of opportunities to practice compassion in small and immediate ways. A bag lady on the corner, a panhandler on the subway, a child in tears, a news account of war, or a local disaster—everyday suffering can crack open our hearts if we let it. In *The Tibetan Book of Living and Dying* the Tibetan Buddhist master Sogyal Rinpoche suggests how to work with these encounters:

> *Don't waste the love and grief [that suffering] arouses; in the moment you feel compassion welling up in you, don't brush it aside, don't shrug it off and try quickly to return to "normal," don't be afraid of your feeling or embarrassed by it, or allow yourself to be distracted from it or let it run aground in apathy. Be vulnerable: use that quick, bright uprush of compassion; focus on it, go deep into your heart and meditate on it, develop it, enhance and deepen it. By doing this you will realize how blind you have been to suffering, how the pain that you are experiencing or seeing now is only a tiny fraction of the pain of the world.*

The Buddha's aspirations for developing compassion provide another exercise to help us deal with the pain of the world. Try repeating the phrase *May you be free of pain and suffering* or *May you be free of pain and sorrow* as you sit in meditation, or whenever you see or think of people in distress during the course of the day. This is an effective practice for opening your heart.

Try This: Giving and Taking

Begin by sitting down in front of a large mirror in which you can see yourself clearly. The person in the mirror is your biographical self, with all its sadness, fears, and difficulties; the person looking at your biological self is the Christ in you, fearless, all loving, calm, awake. See clearly from your Christ-self all your biological self's weaknesses and needs; do not judge them, but see them all without shame, and with detached compassion.

Now imagine that all the fears and needs and desolations your biographical self is harboring issue from the stomach of the image in the mirror in the form of a ball of black smoke. Visualize this ball of black smoke clearly. Then breathe the ball of black smoke into your open and calm Christ-heart, and imagine it dissolving there completely, as smoke would in a cloudless, shining blue sky. Breathe back at your biological self all the peace, bliss, joy, and healing power of your inner Christ.

Do this at least nine times, very calmly and with great concentration. Do not begin breathing back to the self in the mirror the Christ-light until you have seen that the black smoke has dissolved completely in the sky of the heart and nothing but sky remains.

When you feel calm and strong in your Christ-nature, turn with faith and joy to the second part of the practice. Select a person you know who is in psychological or physical pain. Imagine them clearly in your heart's eye, and meditate for a few moments on all the difficulties they must be experiencing and all the grief and fear they must be undergoing.

Now imagine that all their psychological or physical anguish comes out of their stomach in the form of a black ball of smoke. As you breathe in, breathe in that black ball of smoke, and as you breathe out, imagine that you are breathing out the divine light of Christ to the person you are concerned for. Imagine the person completely irradiated by it, and healed of everything that afflicts them.

In the third part of the practice, turn your heart to confront the agony of the whole planet. Imagine the animals dying in the burning forests, the women and children murdered in wars, the horror of the lives of the poor on each continent. Imagine now that the whole earth gives off a ball of black smoke, in which these horrors are concentrated. Breathe in the earth's black smoke, and imagine it dissolving utterly in your heart: breathe out the light

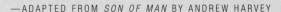

Transmuting Suffering

But what about the mean, frightened, jealous, insensitive people we encounter in our daily lives—or even our own dark feelings? How can we summon up compassion for those people and for ourselves? *Tonglen*, a Tibetan Buddhist practice, offers another way to unblock your heart and change your attitude toward suffering. Though considered an advanced teaching, *tonglen* is for anyone with a sincere desire to root out his or her own selfishness.

Tonglen involves taking in others' suffering with each in-breath, then sending them healing or relief or well-being on the exhale. Pema Chödrön, an American Buddhist nun known for her teachings on compassion, says that *tonglen* practice is about "cultivating fearlessness," because it means making ourselves vulnerable to our own pain.

Traditionally, you practice *tonglen* for someone you know and would like to help. But if, as often happens, you encounter your own fear or anger or resistance, then you can switch to doing *tonglen* for yourself and others who are suffering the same sort of emotional upset. In *When Things Fall Apart* Pema Chödrön explains:

> At that point we can change the focus and begin to do tonglen *for what we are feeling and for millions of other people just like us who at that very moment are feeling exactly the same stuckness and misery. Maybe we are able to name our pain. We recognize it clearly as terror or revulsion or anger or wanting to get revenge. So we breathe in for all the people who are caught with*

the same emotion, and we send out relief or whatever opens up the space for ourselves and all
those countless others. Maybe we can't name what we're feeling. But we can feel it—a tightness
in the stomach, a heavy darkness, or whatever. We simply contact what we are feeling and breathe
in, take it in, for all of us—and send out relief to all of us.

Tonglen invites us to connect with our innate capacity to heal ourselves and others.
The idea that we all have this ability is central to every spiritual tradition. Think of
Christianity. Jesus, one of the world's master healers, offers inspiration for transmut-
ing the pain of human sorrow. The mystical scholar and poet Andrew Harvey has
adapted *tonglen* to help us connect with the compassionate Christ-power that resides in
each of us (see "Giving and Taking," page 100). "If done with sincerity and faith,"
Harvey writes in *Son of Man*, his book about Jesus as a mystic who guides seekers to
their own innate divinity, this practice can "make you a powerful agent of divine
healing in the world."

When we practice giving-and-taking, whether in a formal meditation or as we go
about our daily lives, we begin to feel more loving and no longer so powerless in the
face of human suffering. Sending-and-receiving is a positive action that transforms our
attitudes and behavior toward all beings. Since every action has a reaction, when we extend ourselves to others they blossom, like flowers unfolding in the warmth of the sun.

Inspiration: Tonglen *and the Power of Compassion*

Of all the practices I know, the practice of *tonglen* . . . is one of the most useful and powerful. When you feel yourself locked in upon yourself, *tonglen* opens you to the truth of the
suffering of others; when your heart is blocked it destroys those forces that are obstructing
it; and when you feel estranged from the person who is in pain before you, or bitter or
despairing, it helps you to find within yourself and then to reveal the loving, expansive
radiance of your own true nature. . . . Put very simply, the *tonglen* practice of giving
and receiving is to take on the suffering and pain of others, and give them your happiness,
well-being, and peace of mind.

—SOGYAL RINPOCHE, *THE TIBETAN BOOK OF LIVING AND DYING*

BOOKS

Borysenko, Joan. *The Ways of the Mystic.* Carlsbad, Cal.: Hay House, 1997.

Casarjian, Robin. *Forgiveness.* New York: Bantam, 1992.

Chödrön, Pema. *Start Where You Are.* Boston: Shambhala, 1994.

————. *When Things Fall Apart.* Boston: Shambhala, 1997.

————. *The Wisdom of No Escape.* Boston: Shambhala, 1991.

Cooper, Rabbi David. *Silence, Simplicity, and Solitude.* Woodstock, Vt.: Skylight Paths, 1999.

A Course in Miracles. Mill Valley, Cal. Foundation for Inner Peace, 1975.

Dalai Lama, His Holiness the. *Ocean of Wisdom.* Santa Fe, N.M.: Clear Light, 1989.

Das, Surya, Lama. *Awakening to the Sacred.* New York: Broadway, 1999.

de Mello, Anthony. *Sadhana: A Way to God.* Liguouri, Mo.: Liguouri/Triumph, 1978.

Harvey, Andrew. *Son of Man.* New York: Tarcher, 1998.

Lesser, Elizabeth. *The New American Spirituality.* New York: Random House, 1999.

Nhat Hahn, Thich. *Cultivating the Mind of Love.* Berkeley: Parallax Press, 1996.

————. *Teachings on Love.* Berkeley: Parallax Press, 1997.

Salzberg, Sharon. *A Heart as Wide as the World.* Boston: Shambhala, 1997.

————. *Lovingkindness.* Boston: Shambhala, 1997.

Sogyal Rinpoche. *The Tibetan Book of Living and Dying.* San Francisco: Harper San Francisco, 1992.

Teresa, Mother. *No Greater Love.* Novato, Cal.: New World Library, 1997.

AUDIO/VIDEO

The Art of Forgiving. Robin Casarjian. A practical path to maturity and inner peace (Sounds True).

Awakening Compassion. Pema Chödrön. Meditation practice for difficult times (Sounds True).

Embracing Life Through Lovingkindness. Jack Kornfield. Advice on healing self and others from the founder of Spirit Rock Meditation Center (New Dimensions).

Good Medicine. Pema Chödrön. How to turn pain into compassion with *tonglen* meditation (Sounds True). VHS

Lovingkindness Meditation. Sharon Salzberg. Sounds True. A six-stage meditation for inner healing, from a founder of Insight Meditation Center (Sounds True).

Noble Heart. Pema Chödrön. A self-guided retreat on befriending obstacles (Sounds True).

Seventy Times Seven: On the Spiritual Art of Forgiveness. Joan Borysenko. Practical steps for growing through forgiving self and others (Sounds True).

Son of Man. Andrew Harvey. The mystical path to Christ (Sounds True).

Tibetan Wisdom for Living and Dying. Sogyal Rinpoche. Insights from an ancient tradition on awareness, compassion, and truth (Sounds True).

7.
Meditative
Prayer

You pray in your distress and in your need:
would that you might pray also in the fullness
of your joy and in your days of abundance.
—KAHLIL GIBRAN

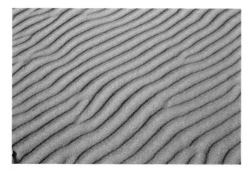

Prayer is found in every culture and faith tradition. The impulse to connect with, or draw on, a spiritual source is fundamentally human. It may even be hard-wired in our brains.

Jungian analyst Ann Ulanov and her husband, Barry, an English professor and lecturer on psychiatry and religion, call prayer "primary speech," a language of images and feelings that originates in "primary-process"—preverbal—thinking. It is an instinctual voice, sounding in our depths from infancy, they explain in *Primary Speech: A Psychology of Prayer*. As adults, our prayers are often driven by those same basic forces. "We are pushed to our knees by an instinct of fright, a desperate cry for help, or an overflowing need to reach out to something we sense is there." Prayer, in short, is a cry from the soul. "Everybody prays," the Ulanovs state, "whether or not they call it prayer":

> We pray every time we ask for help, understanding, or strength, in or out of religion. . . . And even if we do not pray to the God of Scripture or traditional religion, still, every time we call for help or understanding from forces beyond us, we pray to something that one way or another seems to respond to us in terms of our humanity.

Prayer is not just talking to God; listening is an integral part of it. If we don't have our ears and hearts open, how can we hear a response to our entreaties or be conduits for the divine? "What we thought was *our* prayer, *our* effort to pray, reveals itself as God's praying through us," the Ulanovs state.

True prayer, then, involves an exchange. The idea of praying as a conversation with God predates Neale Donald Walsch's best-selling books by several thousand years. One of the first to describe prayer in that way was St. Clement of Alexandria, a member of the early Christian sect known as the Gnostics (from *gnosis*, Greek for "knowledge"), who sought direct awareness of the God within through meditation and prayer.

This view of prayer as a dialogue with the divine is the underpinning of Western spirituality. But if you recoil from praying because of bad childhood memories (sitting on a hard bench in a drafty church or synagogue; endlessly reciting the catechism; listening to hours of religious instruction), or from a fear that nobody's listening anyway, perhaps it's time to form some new ideas about prayer. Prayer can be "thinking out loud"—a way to approach daily life from a broader perspective, so that we can see the deeper meaning of even the most painful experiences. Prayer can help us develop empathy: when you "walk a mile in another's moccasins," you are far less likely to judge his or her actions harshly. Prayer can change our values, instilling in us a stronger sense of right and wrong. Prayer can help us forgive ourselves by connecting us to a forgiving God.

Consider these holy conversations:

◆ While in prison for plotting to overthrow Adolf Hitler, a young German pastor, Dietrich Bonhoeffer, offers a Christmas prayer for his fellow inmates: "Oh, God, early in the morning I cry to you. . . . I am feeble in heart, but with you there is help. I am restless, but with you there is peace. . . . I do not understand your ways, but you know the way for me."

+ The nineteenth-century Danish philosopher Søren Kierkegaard, who struggled all his life with faith, admits to God: "I still do some stupid or imprudent things, and I am at the point of losing courage, thinking that now even everything is lost, and then afterward I understand that exactly this stupidity Thou has turned into infinite wisdom."

+ The warrior Arjuna, in the *Bhagavad-Gita*, the great Hindu *Song of God*, entreats the deity Krishna: ". . . tell me how can we hope to be happy slaying the sons of Dhritarashtra? . . . Where is the joy in the killing of kinsmen?"

+ A Lakota Sioux humbly asks Great Grandfather Spirit: "Fill us with the Light./Give us the strength to understand, and the eye to see./Teach us to walk the soft earth as relatives to all that live."

Prayer is what we all turn to in crisis. There are no atheists in foxholes, according to an old saw. As a twelve-step-program text puts it, "Almost the only scoffers at prayer are those who never tried it enough."

Prayer is not just for times of desperation, however. It can also be a celebration—an expression of joy, a mark of devotion. Like the thirteenth-century Persian poet Rumi (the best-selling poet in America today), or the sixteenth-century Spanish saint Teresa of Avila, or the nineteenth-century Hasidic rabbi Nachman of Breslov, mystics

Inspiration: Prayer for Serenity

God,
grant me
the serenity to accept the things I cannot change,
courage to change the things I can,
and wisdom to know the difference.
Living one day at a time,
enjoying one moment at a time;
accepting hardship as a pathway to peace;
taking, as Jesus did, this sinful world as it is,
not as I would have it;
trusting that You will make all things right
if I surrender to Your will,
so that I may be reasonably happy in this life
and supremely happy with You forever in the next.

—ATTRIBUTED TO THEOLOGIAN REINHOLD NIEBUHR

down through the centuries have been drunk with love for the divine, and unabashed in their outpourings. Sufi dancing is prayer—or meditation—in motion. Drumming, singing hymns, chanting, and the repetition of mantras—sacred phrases—fall somewhere between meditation and prayer. All these practices center our focus and anchor us in the sacred. Along with reading and reflecting on holy verses, reciting prayers, and contemplating sacred icons and images, they are time-honored ways to relate to the divine (see Chapter 8, "Celebrating Your Devotion," and Chapter 9, "Moving with Spirit"). Ultimately, how we worship is intensely personal. We tailor our prayer styles to our personalities or to something deeper—an intangible "pull" of the soul toward sacred union.

Inspiration: Prayer

To pray is to change. This is a great grace. How good of God to provide a path whereby our lives can be taken over by love and joy and peace and patience and kindness and goodness and faithfulness and gentleness and self-control.

—RICHARD J. FOSTER, *PRAYER: FINDING THE HEART'S TRUE HOME*

How, Then, Shall We Pray?

It is often said that there are as many different ways of praying as there are people who pray. Traditionally, most prayers fall into one of three categories: praise, petition, or thanksgiving. We may ask for forgiveness or blessing, seek help or healing for ourselves or others, offer gratitude for what we have received, or simply request knowledge of God's will for us. Sometimes the best we can do is pray to overcome doubt—or to become willing to pray.

A recent Gallup poll found that 90 percent of Americans pray, 75 percent of them every day. More than half the people who pray regularly use that time for a personal chat with God, while 15 percent prefer to repeat familiar prayers—words that have inspired the devout in the past. The renowed Lutheran theologian Martin Marty admits that he is uncomfortable improvising prayer. In *Breaking Through God's Silence* author David Yount recounts Marty's method: "I hitchhike using the vehicles, the instruments, of people who are better at devotion than I am," Marty explains. "I spend a lot of time with anthologies of prayer, with quotations, sourcebooks."

Over the centuries, the spiritually committed in nearly every tradition have served as examples of how to pray and have left us a body of prayers to get us started. Jesus prayed often and gave many instructions on praying, but he taught the disciples the words to only one prayer—the Lord's Prayer, otherwise known as the "Our Father" (see page 110). It is one of the best-known and most enduring prayers in the world.

Whether you create your own prayers, borrow the words of others, or simply sit silently in reverent anticipation is not important, experts say. The key to prayer is your intention: Are you willing to open yourself to a relationship with the Absolute? By all accounts, we do not have to search for God; God is always looking for us. "When you are invited to pray, you are asked to open your tightly clenched fists," the Catholic priest Henri J. M. Nouwen explains in *With Open Hands*. Here's how he suggests bringing prayer into your life:

Prayer is no easy matter. It demands a relationship in which you allow someone other than yourself to enter into the very center of your being, to see there what you would rather leave in darkness, and to touch there what you would rather leave untouched. . . . When you want to pray, then, the first question is: How do I open my closed hands? *. . . Don't be afraid to offer your hate, bitterness, disappointment, to the One who is love and only love. . . . Each time you dare to*

Inspiration: *The Lord's Prayer*

After this manner, therefore pray ye:
Our father which art in heaven,
Hallowed be thy name.
Thy kingdom come.
Thy will be done in earth,
as it is in heaven.
Give us this day our daily bread,
And forgive us our debts,
as we forgive our debtors'.
And lead us not into temptation,
but deliver us from evil:
For thine is the kingdom,
and the power, and the glory,
for ever. Amen.

—MATTHEW 6: 9–13 (KJV)

let go and surrender one of those many fears, your hand opens a little and your palms spread out in a gesture of receiving.

There are those, like the Vietnamese Zen master Thich Nhat Hanh, who stress that how we live our daily lives shows our connection with the divine—every breath is a prayer. Brother Lawrence, a seventeenth-century French Carmelite monk, found formal prayer impossible; in *The Practice of the Presence of God*—a classic of mystical literature— he tells us that his solution was to spend every moment in conscious awareness of, or silent conversation with, God. And one of the most important teachings of both Buddhism and the *Kabbalah*—Jewish mysticism—is that everything is connected. Hence, whatever we do in our individual lives influences the whole. Mother Teresa, the Catholic nun who inspired millions with her work among the poor in Calcutta, put it another way: "What we say does not matter, only what God says to souls through us."

In fact, you do not have to "say" anything to pray. In many traditions words are considered inadequate to express the sacred mystery. The *Tao Te Ching*, the great work of Taoism, starts with the statement "The Tao [sacred way] that can be spoken is not the eternal Tao." The ancient Hebrews spelled the name of God only in consonants (YHVH—*yod hey vav hey*—known as the Tetragrammaton) to signify that the name is too holy to be uttered. So we do not have to grope for the right words to be prayerful. "Prayer means above all to be accepting toward God," Henri Nouwen tells us.

Meditative forms of prayer are a powerful way to achieve a deep and personal sacred connection. In *The Presence of Absence* the writer Doris Grumbach recounts her

---

Inspiration: Practicing the Presence

The holiest, most universal, and most necessary practice in the spiritual life is the presence of God. To practice the presence of God is to take pleasure in and become accustomed to His Divine company, speaking humbly and conversing lovingly in our hearts with Him at all times, and at every moment, especially in times of temptation, pain, spiritual dryness, revulsion to spiritual things, and even unfaithfulness and sin.

—BROTHER LAWRENCE, *THE PRACTICE OF THE PRESENCE OF GOD*

efforts, through a practice she calls "nondiscursive prayer," to recapture the immediacy of God she had experienced as a young woman fifty years before:

> *I had discovered how necessary it was (for me) to discard my stale concepts of God and ritual practices in order to approach the pure core of prayer. A long life in the church had formed me into a halfhearted, secular worshiper.*

Grumbach's experience is hauntingly familiar to anyone caught between "public" and "private" spiritual life, unable to find adequate sustenance from traditional services in church, temple, or mosque. "For someone like me," she explains, "faith is not linear, a display, moving from the individual into the world beyond, but rather circular and centering, revolving around the hope of a hungry soul to meet up with God. . . ." (See "Intention and Prayer," below.)

Inspiration: Intention and Prayer

My practice in contemplation, during the few minutes after the reading of a psalm or psalms, was to use for reflection phrases or sentences that had captivated me. I erased all visions of the old, anthropomorphic view of God which now and then crept into my view and cleared away everything except the suggestions that arose from the words themselves.

At first the sentence or sentences I seemed to choose were instructions for my patience. Wait for Him, be patient with His absence, sit still, do not fill His absence with useless disquietude. . . . I developed a curious practice in my moments of waiting to which I gave the name of prayer, nondiscursive prayer. In the blackness behind my closed eyelids I projected a small square in which were enclosed the words I was contemplating. . . . I then moved the words out of the square, leaving blackness enclosed in blackness. . . . I tried to extend the period of nothingness each time, believing that as long as I was without words there was a chance that the sense of God's presence might come to fill completely the wordless void. Blank intention was the prayer.

—DORIS GRUMBACH, *THE PRESENCE OF ABSENCE*

The Contemplative Tradition

Most of us associate meditation with the East and prayer with the West. But Christian and Jewish mystical practices contain elements of both prayer and meditation. "The root of prayer is interior silence," declares Father Thomas Keating, a Trappist monk at St. Benedict's monastery in Snowmass, Colorado, who has written extensively about prayer and spirituality.

Contemplative prayer has deep roots in Judeo-Christian tradition. In the spiritual melting pot of the ancient Near East, Jewish mystics and early Christians developed prayer lives that centered on meditation and contemplative practices. (The Catholic Church defines *meditation* as "reflecting on a sacred text," and *contemplation* as "the state of resting in God's presence."

Contemplative prayer is the essence of monastic life. It was practiced in the fourth and fifth centuries by the Desert Fathers and Mothers—hermits and ascetics living in remote parts of Egypt, Arabia, Persia, and Palestine, who sought a direct, heartfelt connection with God. In the centuries since, monks and mystics such as Meister Eckhart, Julian of Norwich, Teresa of Avila, and John of the Cross, as well as twentieth-century clerics such as Thomas Merton and Henri Nouwen, have kept the contemplative tradition alive. Their writings continue to inspire anyone interested in spiritual life. We learn of the *via positiva* and its ecstatic states of mystical union, as well as the challenges of the *via negativa*—the sometimes rocky spiritual road that strips the seeker of ego and other attachments that stand in God's way.

Jewish mystical tradition predates Christianity, but not until the Middle Ages do written records emerge. A handful of mystics—from medieval Kabbalists such as Abraham Abulafia, Joseph Ibn Paluda, and Moses de León to the founder of Ha-

Inspiration: Contemplation

Contemplation is a sudden gift of awareness, an awakening to the Real within all that is real.

—THOMAS MERTON, *NEW SEEDS OF CONTEMPLATION*

sidism, Isaac Luria (known as the Baal Shem Tov), and his great-grandson, Rabbi Nachman of Breslov—elaborated on ancient contemplative practices to devise methods for achieving transcendent states and oneness with God.

From the beginning Americans were drawn to mysticism; the colonists were open to everything from trance to ecstatic whirling. Esoteric traditions such as Freemasonry, a philosophy of ethical conduct celebrating social justice, influenced the Founding Fathers and were woven into the fabric of the American Constitution. In *The New American Spirituality* Elizabeth Lesser observes that the eclectic and self-styled spiritual paths many seekers are following today reflect fundamental American values—democracy, diversity, and respect for individual rights. In piecing together spiritual lives from a variety of sources, we are the true heirs of our inquiring and open-minded ancestors.

In the nineteenth century, Asian philosophies—particularly Hindu texts such as the *Bhagavad-Gita* and, to a lesser extent, the writings of Confucius and the Sufi poets—captivated progressive thinkers such as Henry Thoreau, Ralph Waldo Emerson, and the other Transcendentalists. The first World Parliament of Religions, held in Chicago in 1893, introduced a wider audience to Eastern thought. Over the next half century interest in Eastern spiritual practices grew, and the writings of the Christian mystics were rediscovered.

The Second Vatican Council, convened under Pope John XXIII in the mid-1960s, called for spiritual renewal, opening the door to a resurgence of contemplative practice. However, many young Catholics, like their Protestant and Jewish contemporaries, were already leaving the church in favor of Eastern meditative disciplines that offered a more direct connection to spirit.

This explosion of interest in meditation was followed by a period of cross-fertilization, as leaders in every faith sought to reengage their congregations. Today's spiritual seekers can look to either the East or the West for practices that foster an intimate relationship with God. Many of us are drawing from both.

Contact with Eastern contemplative philosophies is changing the way many people view prayer. Physician Larry Dossey, who writes widely about the scientifically demonstrated healing effects of prayer, points out there is quite a difference between Western prayer, which generally addresses a God *out there*—or *up* there—and Eastern prayer, in which the divine is envisaged as inside each of us and inseparable from all existence, simultaneously everywhere and nowhere, beyond cause and effect. When

God is not externalized, Dossey notes, prayer becomes less a petition for divine intervention to meet our personal agendas and more a means of entering the sacred stream of life.

"Prayer is not doing, but being," the author Kathleen Norris writes in *Amazing Grace*. "It is not words but the beyond-words experience of coming into the presence of something much greater than oneself."

Conversing with God

Children are natural mystics. In childhood, we talk to God as easily as we talk to the spirits of the trees, the wind, the stones, the sea. Spirits are as real to us as our parents or pets or imaginary playmates, and we feel no self-consciousness in carrying on elaborate conversations with the unseen. Exploring the great mystery of life is simply an extension of that childhood curiosity about how things work, Rabbi David L. Cooper suggests in *God Is a Verb*. Mystical Judaism is one tradition that emphasizes a personal connection with, an ongoing conversation with, God.

Jewish mystical practices are hidden treasures, found in Kabbalistic and Hasidic teachings that for centuries were passed on in secret, mostly orally. The late Rabbi Aryeh Kaplan, whose translations introduced Jewish mysticism to many modern seekers, traced the roots of Jewish spontaneous prayer and meditation all the way back to Abraham's dialogues with God. Unstructured "oral conversation" is well documented from ancient times, he states in *Jewish Meditation*. Rabbi Nachman of Breslov made oral conversation a core of his teaching. To start the conversational ball rolling, Rabbi Nachman suggested repeating, *Ribbono shel Olam*—"Master of the Universe"—until other words spontaneously followed (see "Talking with God," above).

Like Moses on the mountain Jewish mystics historically withdrew into solitude (*hitbodedut*) to commune with God. Rabbi Nachman sent his students into nature for their conversations, but Rabbi Cooper suggests that it is possible to find the inner silence for talking to God even in the midst of a busy city street.

The word *Kabbalah*, Cooper points out, comes from the root *kbl*, "to receive." The *Kabbalah* teaches that through "contemplative observation" we can receive direct insight into the unity of all creation. Unlike Eastern traditions, which see reality as monolithic and our perception of duality (I and other, subject and object) as illusion, the Kabbalistic view is that reality exists on many levels simultaneously. The vaster our awareness, the more clearly we can see these multiple levels of experience, at the same time that we are moving toward union with "the Divine Oneness."

This expanded awareness is called *mochin de gadlut*—"mind of bigness"—Cooper explains. Kabbalah offers many ways to expand our awareness and merge with God. The Shema, or Sh'ma—*Shema Yisrael, Adonai Eloheinu, Adonai Echad* ("Hear, O Israel, the

Try This: The Shema Prayer

"Daily meditation on the Shema is the mainstay of Kabbalistic prayer," writes Perle Besserman in *The Shambhala Guide to Kabbalah and Jewish Mysticism.* The following instructions are based on her suggestions.

1. Sit in a meditation posture on a chair or floor cushion, with your eyes closed and your breathing relaxed.
2. Silently recite the phrase *Shema Yisrael Adonai Eloheinu Adonai Echad* ("Hear, O Israel, the Lord our God, the Lord is One").
3. When you are totally focused on the Shema, begin matching the words to your breathing, using one complete breath—inhalation and exhalation—for each word.
4. Next, concentrate on *Echad* (pronounced Eh-had)—"One"—dwelling on it twice as long as on the other words in the phrase.
5. Continue concentrating on *Echad* until you are no longer consciously articulating the word but are "breathing" it.
6. After twenty-five minutes, close your meditation by reciting *Baruch shem kevod malkhuto le-olam va-ed* ("Blessed be the Name of the Glory of His kingdom forever and ever").

Lord Our God, the Lord is One")—is the main vehicle for this ("The Shema Prayer," above). Observant Jews say this prayer in the morning and at night, but you don't have to be Jewish to have a powerful experience from reciting it, Rabbi Cooper assures us. The words were delivered by Moses to the Israelites along with the Ten Commandments, and according to St. Mark, Jesus repeated them when he was asked which commandment was the most important. Thus, the Shema connects both Jew and non-Jew "with a common inner essence that longs to be at one with the source of creation," Rabbi Cooper writes in *God Is a Verb.*

Contemplative Prayer

Whether you call it meditation or contemplative prayer, the discipline of quieting the body, focusing the mind, and opening the heart to the divine holds out the promise of spiritual transformation. Trappist monk Thomas Merton tells us in *Contemplative Prayer* that prayer begins with "finding one's deepest center, awakening the profound depths of our being in the presence of God, who is the source of our being and our life." Prayer of this sort, Merton adds, "seeks its roots in the very ground of our being, not merely in our mind or our affections."

The essence of the contemplative tradition is what Pope Gregory the Great, fourteen centuries ago, called "resting in God." How do we reach that place? What path can we follow to our inner core? Centering prayer is one way, suggests Thomas Keating, who is a founder of the Centering Prayer movement and of Contemplative Outreach, an ecumenical organization that encourages the practice of contemplative prayer.

Back in the 1970s, while he was abbot of St. Joseph's Abbey in Spencer, Massachusetts, Keating and two fellow monks began offering Christian retreats that incorporated elements of Eastern spiritual practice, particularly meditation. Out of that experience they developed centering prayer as a way to deepen the individual's relationship with God. In *Open Mind, Open Heart* Keating sums up its purpose:

Jesus said, "Watch and pray." This is what we are doing in centering prayer. Watching is just enough activity to stay alert. Praying is opening to God.

Inspiration: What Is Contemplative Prayer?

Contemplative prayer is not so much the absence of thoughts as detachment from them. It is the opening of mind and heart, body and emotions—our whole being—to God, the Ultimate Mystery, beyond words, thoughts, and emotions. . . .

—THOMAS KEATING, *OPEN MIND, OPEN HEART*

Centering prayer is based on a method suggested by an unknown fourteenth-century English mystic in *The Cloud of Unknowing*, a classic work on contemplative practice. It involves sitting quietly and concentrating on a sacred name or inspirational word, to "soften" ourselves for God's presence. Once the intention to receive God feels firmly established, you can stop repeating the word and simply sit.

Possible words to repeat include *Lord, Jesus, Father, Abba* (Aramaic for "Dad"), *Mother, Mary, Peace, Love,* or *Yes.* Non-Christians might choose a name or word evocative of their own tradition, such as *Grandfather, Allah, Goddess, Gaia, Echad* ("One" in Hebrew), or *Shalom.* (Christian Meditation, a similar practice developed in the 1970s by John Main, an Irish-English Benedictine monk who had studied in India, draws on the early Christian practice of using the word *Maranatha,* Aramaic for "Come, Lord." In Christian Meditation the word is repeated continuously, as a mantra, for the duration of the practice period, usually twenty to thirty minutes.)

Keating sets out four simple steps for practicing Centering Prayer that can be used by anyone, regardless of spiritual belief (see "Guidelines for Centering Prayer," below). He calls contemplative prayer "divine psychotherapy." More than just a spiritual exercise, it is a way of "unloading"—clearing the unconscious of painful memories, dark desires, and traumas to allow grace to enter our lives. In the silence and stillness of meditative prayer we can descend beneath the false self we create to hide our fears

Try This: Guidelines for Centering Prayer

1. Choose a sacred word as the symbol of your intention to consent to God's presence and action within.
2. Sitting comfortably and with eyes closed, settle briefly, and silently introduce the sacred word as the symbol of your consent to God's presence and action within.
3. When you become aware of thoughts, return ever so gently to the sacred word.
4. At the end of the prayer period, remain in silence with eyes closed for a couple of minutes.

—THOMAS KEATING, *INTIMACY WITH GOD*

and flaws, and can excavate and release emotional blocks. "The psyche as well as the body has its way of evacuating material that is harmful to its health," Keating notes in *Open Mind, Open Heart.*

Listening for God

Spiritually, centering prayer owes much to the practice of *lectio divina* ("divine reading"), which dates back to the birth of Christian monasticism in the fourth century. It is a way of inviting a "personal meeting with the Lord," as the Trappist monk M. Basil Pennington explains in *Awake in the Spirit.* The process involves reading a short passage of scripture and "listening" to it—savoring it—as if God were speaking through it *(lectio)*, then taking a word or phrase and dwelling on it until it "drops" from the head to the heart *(meditatio)* and a response spontaneously emerges *(oratio)*. The final stage *(contemplatio)* is resting in God's presence.

Reflecting on sacred texts or stories is a time-honored way to open up to higher wisdom in many traditions. The Sufis—mystics with roots in Islam—are masters of the teaching story. Like Zen stories Sufi tales can be as witty as they are wise; they enlighten by shifting our perspective. Teaching stories often center on a familiar

Inspiration: *The Fool*

A philosopher, having made an appointment to dispute with Nasrudin, called and found him away from home. Infuriated, he picked up a piece of chalk and wrote, *Stupid Oaf,* on Nasrudin's gate. As soon as he got home and saw this, [Nasrudin] rushed to the philosopher's house.

"I had forgotten," he said, "that you were to call. And I apologize for not having been at home. Of course, I remembered the appointment as soon as I saw that you had left your name on my door."

—INDRIES SHAH, *THE EXPLOITS OF THE INCOMPARABLE NASRUDIN*

character found across cultures—the "holy fool," who defies convention and mirrors our humanity. Nasrudin is a universally loved example (see "The Fool," page 120).

The late Anthony de Mello, a popular Jesuit retreat leader, often gave retreatants what he called "story meditations"—short tales for contemplation to help them connect with their own inner wisdom. In *Taking Flight* de Mello passes along advice from the author of the ancient Hindu epic poem *The Mahabharata:* "If you listen carefully to a story you will never be the same again. That is because the story will worm its way into your heart and break down barriers to the divine."

That is the essence of meditative prayer: It enables us to come to rest in the heart and open ourselves to receive the divine.

Pray Without Ceasing

The image of prayer as an inner journey toward God is a familiar one. "In prayer we are constantly on the way, on pilgrimage," Henri Nouwen observes in *With Open Hands.* "On our way we meet more and more people who show us something about the God whom we seek."

One such tale that has inspired many modern seekers is *The Way of the Pilgrim.* With

---

Try This: Pray Without Ceasing

The unceasing, interior Jesus prayer is the uninterrupted, continual calling upon the divine name of Jesus Christ, with the lips, the mind, and the heart, while calling to mind His constant presence and beseeching His mercy, during any activity one may be occupied with, in all places, at all times, and even while sleeping. The words of this prayer are as follows: "Lord Jesus Christ, have mercy on me!" If one makes a habit of this supplication, one will experience great comfort and a need to repeat this prayer unceasingly, so that eventually one will not be able to live without it and the prayer will flow of its own accord.

—*THE WAY OF THE PILGRIM*, TRANS. BY OLGA SAVIN

its companion volume, *The Pilgrim Continues His Way*, it follows the journey of the author, an unknown nineteenth-century Russian pilgrim who aspires to live by St. Paul's injunction to the Thessalonians: "Pray without ceasing." The pilgrim meets up with a *starets*—an Eastern Orthodox holy man—who instructs him to silently repeat the Jesus prayer: "Lord Jesus, have mercy on me." Known as the "Prayer of the Heart," it comes from the Philokalia, an important collection of Eastern Christian writings dating from the fourth to the fourteenth centuries. (*Philokalia* means "the love of good.") The Jesus Prayer and *The Way of the Pilgrim* were what Franny Glass (to her mother's consternation) found so compelling in J. D. Salinger's novel *Franny and Zooey*.

Hesychasm—this method of praying by silently repeating a phrase over and over as you gradually take its meaning into your heart—originated with the early Christians. The basis of Eastern Orthodox mysticism, the process is transformative. Just as in meditation thoughts and thinker become one, in hesychasm separation between the prayer and the pray-er eventually ceases. The prayer becomes like background music playing constantly in the pray-er's mind and heart.

Power Prayers and Pray-ers

Nearly everyone has a favorite prayer, and this chapter contains a few of the classics that have provided inspiration in various cultures. We can also learn a lot from the world's "power pray-ers." As Henri Nouwen said, they show us something about the God we seek. They also show us something about ourselves.

Take St. Augustine, a fourth-century convert to Christianity. At thirty-two he was baptized, abandoning fast-track ambitions and a life of excess. A decade later, by then a bishop of Hippo, a North African seaport, he spent a year writing his autobiography. *The Confessions* are an astonishing account of spiritual awakening in the form of a sustained conversation with God. "Let me know you, O you who know me; then shall I know even as I am known," Augustine entreats. "Why then am I relating all this to you at such length?" he later wonders. "I do it to arouse my own loving devotion toward you, and that of my readers, so that together we may declare, *Great is the Lord, and exceedingly worthy of praise.*"

Then there is St. Teresa of Avila. A passionate and revolutionary sixteenth-century Spanish mystic, Teresa "was born with a warrior's heart locked inside a woman's body," as Mother Tessa Bielecki tells us in her foreword to *Teresa of Avila*, a collection of the saint's writings. The book's subtitle, "Ecstasy and Common Sense," aptly describes Teresa's extremes of spiritual unfolding. From a privileged childhood she fled to the convent at twenty, then for the next forty-seven years pursued "divine intimacy" with famous intensity, founding the Carmelite order with the assistance of St. John of the Cross and her band of spiritual "conquistadors," as Mother Tessa dubbed them. Teresa saw prayer as the means of "watering a garden" that God has already planted for us, and exhorted us to "take no notice of that feeling you get of wanting to leave off in the middle of your prayer, but praise the Lord for the desire you have to pray...."

Spiritual leaders as diverse as the Dalai Lama and Pope John Paul II draw on the wisdom of another master pray-er, Meister Eckhart, an early fourteenth-century German Dominican priest. Eckhart's oft-quoted observation about our inseparable connection to the Divine is: "The eye by which I see God is the same as the eye by which God sees me." Indeed, the underlying idea of Eckhart's thoughts on prayer could have come from either East or West. In *Table Talk*, excerpted in the anthology *Meister Eckhart, from Whom God Hid Nothing*, he writes:

> *The most powerful prayer, one well nigh omnipotent, and the worthiest work of all, is the outcome of a quiet mind.... A quiet mind is one which nothing weighs on, nothing worries, which, free from ties and from all self-seeking, is wholly merged into the will of God and dead to its own.*

Inspiration: Longing for God

Thou awakest us to delight in Thy praises; for Thou madest us for Thyself, and our heart is restless, until it repose in Thee.

—ST. AUGUSTINE, *THE CONFESSIONS*

Making Prayer Personal

For anyone interested in prayer, the literature is rich. There are countless collections of prayers and inspirational readings in all traditions; a few are listed in "Resources," page 126.

You can make your contemplative experience more personal, however, by creating your own prayer book, with prayers, passages, quotes, and verses that are particularly meaningful to you. Look for a bound book with blank pages that you find beautiful and copy the prayers in your best handwriting. A woman who makes paper as a hobby likes to give handmade blank books to friends, inscribing each book with a favorite prayer to bless the recipient. If you are artistic, you might want to decorate the pages of your book, like the illuminated manuscripts of early Hindu, Persian, and Christian texts. The very act of copying prayers into the book is a prayer in itself.

Lama Surya Das, an American-born Tibetan Buddhist who was raised Jewish, takes along his personal prayer book whenever he travels. In *Awakening to the Sacred* he explains:

> *I know the prayers in my book by heart, but for me that little book reverberates with spiritual energy. So start collecting your prayers. They don't all have to be formal prayers. Sometimes we*

Inspiration: Finding the Prayer of Your Heart

To come to an answer to the personal question: "What is the prayer of my heart?" we first of all have to know how to find this most personal prayer. Where do we look, what do we do, to whom do we go, in order to discover how we as individual human beings—with our own history, our own milieu, our own character, our own insights, and our own freedom to act—are called to enter into intimacy with God? The question about the prayer of our heart is, in fact, the question about our own most personal vocation.

—HENRI J.M. NOUWEN, *REACHING OUT*

hear words, phrases, bits of hymns, chants, or even pop songs that speak to us in a very personal and spiritual way.

Ultimately, our prayer books are only another way in—a vehicle to ride to the center of our being, where we communicate directly with the divine. In *Eternal Echoes* the popular Irish Catholic scholar John O'Donohue calls prayer "a bridge between longing and belonging." It often emerges, he suggests, from a sense of wonder, from that place deep within us that is open to the mystery, that delights in the inexplicable adventure of being alive. Prayer, above all, should lead us to joy, O'Donohue emphasizes: "In the silence of our prayer we should be able to sense the roguish smile of a joyful god who, despite all the chaos and imperfection, ultimately shelters everything."

Write your own prayer, O'Donohue challenges us. (See "Create a Prayer of Your Soul," below.) Take a month, even a year, he says, but make it a prayer that truly expresses your essence. Then memorize it, O'Donohue advises, so that you can "carry this gracious prayer around the world with you" as your "mantra companion."

Like the prayer of the heart that the Russian pilgrim prayed without ceasing, your prayer will lay you open to the sacred and transform your being. And, John O'Donohue promises, "It will bring the wild and tender light of your heart to every object, place, and person that you will meet."

Try This: Create a Prayer of Your Soul

Listen to the voices of longing in your soul. Listen to your hungers. Give attention to the unexpected that lives around the rim of your life. Listen to your memory and to the onrush of your future, to the voices of those near you and those you have lost. Out of all that, make a prayer that is big enough for your wild soul, yet tender enough for your shy and awkward vulnerability; that has enough healing to gain the ointment of divine forgiveness for your wounds; enough truth and vigor to challenge your blindness and complacency; enough graciousness and vision to mirror your immortal beauty. Write a prayer that is worthy of the destiny to which you have been called.

—JOHN O'DONOHUE, *ETERNAL ECHOES*

RESOURCES

BOOKS

Appleton, George, ed. *The Oxford Book of Prayer.* New York: Oxford University Press, 1985.

Armstrong, Karen. *Visions of God.* New York: Bantam, 1994.

Augustine, Saint. *The Confessions.* New York: Vintage, 1997.

Avila, St. Teresa of. *Interior Castle.* New York: Image, 1972.

Besserman, Perle. *The Shambhala Guide to Kabbalah and Jewish Mysticism.* Boston: Shambhala, 1997.

The Song of God: Bhagavad-Gita. New York: New American Library, 1993.

The Bible. King James Version.

Bielecki, Mother Tessa. *Teresa of Avila.* Boston: Shambhala, 1996.

Bonhoeffer, Dietrich. *Letters and Papers from Prison.* New York: Macmillan, 1971.

Caine, Kenneth Winston, and Brian Paul Kaufman. *Prayer, Faith, and Healing.* Emmaus, Pa.: Rodale, 1999.

Carse, James P. *The Silence of God.* San Francisco: Harper San Francisco, 1985.

The Cloud of Unknowing and Other Works. Clifton Wolters, trans. New York: Penguin, 1961.

Cooper, Rabbi David L. *God Is a Verb.* New York: Riverhead, 1997.

Das, Lama Surya. *Awakening to the Sacred.* New York: Broadway, 1999.

de Mello, Anthony. *Taking Flight.* New York: Image, 1988.

Dossey, Larry, M.D. *Be Careful What You Pray For . . . You Just Might Get It.* San Francisco: Harper San Francisco, 1997.

———. *Healing Words.* San Francisco: Harper San Francisco, 1993.

———. *Prayer Is Good Medicine.* San Francisco: Harper San Francisco, 1996.

Eckhart, Meister. *Meister Eckhart.* Raymond B. Blakney, trans. New York: Harper Torchbooks, 1941.

———. *Meister Eckhart, from Whom God Hid Nothing.* Boston: Shambhala, 1996.

Epstein, Perle. *Kabbalah: The Way of the Jewish Mystic.* Boston: Shambhala, 1978.

The Essential Rumi. Coleman Barks, trans. San Francisco: Harper San Francisco, 1995.

The Fellowship in Prayer. *The Gift of Prayer: A Treasury of Personal Prayer from the World's Spiritual Traditions.* New York: Continuum, 1997.

Foster, Richard. *Prayer.* San Francisco: Harper San Francisco, 1964.

———. *Streams of Living Water.* San Francisco: Harper San Francisco, 1998.

Gibran, Kahlil. *The Prophet.* New York: Random House, 1997.

Grumbach, Doris. *The Presence of Absence.* Boston: Beacon, 1998.

Harvey, Andrew, ed. *Teachings of the Christian Mystics.* Boston: Shambhala, 1998.

Jones, Timothy. *The Art of Prayer.* New York: Ballantine, 1997.

Julian of Norwich. *Showings.* Mahwah, NJ: Paulist Press, 1978.

Kaplan, Aryeh. *Jewish Meditation.* New York: Schocken, 1985.

Keating, Thomas. *Active Meditations for Contemplative Prayer.* New York: Continuum, 1997.

———. *Intimacy with God.* New York: Crossroad, 1994.

———. *Open Mind, Open Heart.* New York: Continuum, 1986.

Lawrence, Brother. *The Practice of the Presence of God.* Orleans, Mass.: Paraclete Press, 1985.

Leet, Leonara. *Renewing the Convenant.* Rochester, Vt.: Inner Traditions, 1999.

Lefevre, Perry D., ed. *The Prayers of Kierkegaard.* Chicago: The University of Chicago Press, 1965.

Lesser, Elizabeth. *The New American Spirituality.* New York: Random House, 1999.

Mascetti, Manuela Dunn. *Christian Mysticism.* New York: Hyperion, 1998.

Mechthild, of Magdeburg. *Meditations from Mechthild of Magdeburg.* Henry L. Carrigan, Jr., ed. Orleans, Mass.: Paraclete, 1999.

Merton, Thomas. *Contemplative Prayer.* New York: Image, 1969.

Merton, Thomas. *New Seeds of Contemplation.* New York: New Directions, 1961.

Nassal, Reverend Joseph, and Nancy Burke. *How to Pray.* Deerfield Beach, Fl.: Health Communications, 1998.

Norris, Kathleen. *Amazing Grace.* New York: Riverhead, 1998.

Nouwen, Henri J. M. *Reaching Out.* New York: Image, 1975.

———. *With Open Hands.* New York: Ballantine, 1972.

O'Donohue, John. *Eternal Echoes.* New York: Cliff Street Books, 1999.

Pennington, M. Basil. *Awake in the Spirit.* New York: Crossroad, 1992.

Pietsch, William V. *The Serenity Prayer Book.* San Francisco: Harper San Francisco, 1990.

The Prayers of Kierkegaard. Perry D. Lefevre, ed. Chicago: The University of Chicago Press, 1956.

Redmont, Jane. *When in Doubt, Sing.* New York: HarperCollins, 1999.

Reininger, Gustave, ed. *Centering Prayer in Daily Life and Ministry.* New York: Continuum, 1998.

Roberts, Elizabeth, and Elias Amidon. *Life Prayers.* San Francisco: Harper San Francisco, 1996.

—. *Prayers for a Thousand Years.* San Francisco: Harper San Francisco, 1999.

Roth, Ron. *The Healing Path of Prayer.* New York: Harmony, 1999.

Salinger, J.D. *Franny and Zooey.* New York: Bantam, 1955.

Shah, Indries. *The Exploits of the Incomparable Nasrudin.* New York: Dutton, 1966.

Stendl-Rast, Brother David. *Gratefulness: The Heart of Prayer.* Mahwah, NJ: Paulist Press, 1990.

St. John of the Cross. E. Allison Peers, trans. *Dark Night of the Soul.* New York: Image, 1959.

Taylor, Eugene. *Shadow Culture: Psychology and Spirituality in America.* Washington, DC: Counterpoint, 1999.

Mother Teresa. Compiled by Jose Gonzalez-Balado. *Mother Teresa: In My Own Words.* New York: Gramercy, 1996.

Ulanov, Ann and Barry. *Primary Speech: A Psychology of Prayer.* Louisville, Ky.: John Knox Press, 1985.

The Upanishads. New York: New American Library, 1990.

Walsch, Neale Donald. *Conversations with God, Books 1–3.* Charlottesville, Va.: Hampton Roads.

The Way of the Pilgrim and *The Pilgrim Continues His Way.* R. M. French, trans. New York: Ballantine, 1974.

The Way of the Pilgrim. Olga Savin, trans. Boston: Shambhala, 1991.

Yount, David. *Breaking Through God's Silence.* New York: Touchstone, 1996.

PERIODICALS

Christian Meditation USA
Christian Meditation Center
1080 West Irving Park Road
Roselle, IL 60172
(630) 351–2613
quarterly newsletter

Daily Word
Inspirational readings, published by Silent Unity (see ORGANIZATIONS)

Sacred Journey
291 Witherspoon Street
Princeton, NJ 08542–6863
(609) 924–6863
Published bi-monthly by Fellowship in Prayer (see ORGANIZATIONS)

AUDIO/VIDEO

Christian Meditation: The Essential Teachings. Introduction to Christian meditation (Christian Meditation Center).

The Contemplative Journey I & II. Father Thomas Keating. Guide to Christian contemplation, with teachings on Centering Prayer (Sounds True).

East and West: The Mystical Connection: An Overview with Father Bede Griffiths. Reflections of a Western monk who lived for many years in India (New Dimensions).

Eternal Echoes. John O'Donohue. Irish poet and scholar on the yearning to belong (Sounds True).

Eyes Remade for Wonder. Rabbi Lawrence Kushner. Popular rabbi and NPR commentator on Jewish mysticism and spirituality (Sounds True).

The Grateful Heart. Brother David Steindl-Rask. Prayer as a way to open to life's blessings (Sounds True).

The Holy Chariot. Rabbi David A. Cooper. Daily practices on the Jewish mystical path to higher consciousness (Sounds True).

Intercessory Prayer. Reverend Jane E. Vennard. Classical practice for calling on God to help (Sounds True).

Kabbalah. Perle Besserman. Teachings on the way of the Jewish mystic (Sounds True).

Kabbalah Meditation. Rabbi David A. Cooper. Unique meditations to contact higher planes of awareness (Sounds True).

The Lost Mode of Prayer. Gregg Braden. Powerful ancient practices from the Desert Fathers to focus thoughts and emotions (Sounds True).

Love Is a Fire and I Am Wood. Llewelyn Vaughan-Lee. Sufi teachings and prayer (Sounds True).

Morning and Evening Meditations and Prayer. Joan Borysenko. Daily practices to heal body, mind, and soul from a noted psychologist and teacher (Hay House).

The Mystical Kabbalah. Rabbi David A. Cooper. Judaism's ancient systems for exploration through meditation and contemplation (Sounds True).

Passion for God. Mother Tessa Bielecki. A guide to ecstatic prayer and the legacy of the Christian mystic. Saint Teresa of Avila (Sounds True).

Son of Man. Andrew Harvey. Prayers and meditations on the mystical path to Christ (Sounds True).

Tales of Rebbe Nachman. Rabbi David Zeller. Teaching stories for living in God's presence (Sounds True).

Touching the Divine. Wayne Muller. Teachings, meditations, and contemplations to awaken your true nature (Sounds True).

The Tree of Life. Rabbi David Zeller. Meditations, prayers, and practices of Jewish mysticism (Sounds True).

The Way of Saint Francis. Father Murray Bodo. Teachings and practices for daily life, inspired by St. Francis of Assisi's keys to opening inner space (Sounds True).

ORGANIZATIONS

Christian Meditation Center
1080 West Irving Park Road
Roselle, IL 60172
(630) 351–2613

Contemplative Outreach
10 Park Place, Suite 2B
PO Box 737
Butler, NJ 07405
(973) 838–3384

Fellowship in Prayer
291 Witherspoon Street
Princeton, NJ 08542–9946
(609) 924–6863

Heart of Stillness Retreats
PO Box 106
Jamestown, CO 80455
(303) 459–3431

WEB SITES

www.centeringprayer.com

Contemplative Outreach, founded by Father Thomas Keating; includes Centering Prayer program, newsletter, magazine, events calendars, and local contacts.

www.wccm.org

Site of the World Community of Christian Meditation, dedicated to the practice of Christian meditation taught by John Main, OSB. Includes weekly Internet meditation group, on-line newsletters, and more.

www.weewisdom.org

Site of the Unity church headquarters, with daily prayer sessions and continuous prayer vigil.

8.

Celebrating
Your Devotion

O Love, O pure deep Love, be here,
be now. . . .
Make me your servant, your breath, your core.

—JALALUDDIN RUMI

Living a contemplative life doesn't call for a joyless denial of the senses. Quite the opposite. Poetry, art, visualization, chanting, and singing are time-honored ways to express spiritual devotion and celebrate the divine.

Any art form offers a vehicle for contemplation. In a broad sense contemplation means "resting with" God or a higher power or the holy. This communion is the fruit of spiritual practice—the result of whatever method you use to open yourself to the sacred. In their compendium of spiritual practice, *Soul Work*, Anne A. Simpkinson and Charles H. Simpkinson explain that "contemplative practices rely on intention rather than attention, the intention being to surrender all in order to be in the presence of the Divine."

But even practices intended to foster sacred union require attention of some sort. The methods in this chapter involve concentrating on—contemplating—an object, rather than emptying the mind. The object of contemplation may be words or images or sounds. And if you add other sensory input, such as scent (the smell of burning incense, for example) or touch (the cool, smooth feel of prayer beads, perhaps), then even the simplest spiritual practice becomes a rich, evocative experience—a sacred ceremony. "Worship developed before theology did," author Kathleen Norris told an Amazon.com interviewer. "It's actually singing and doing things and celebrating. That comes first and the explanations come later."

What can we do to create these radiant moments?

Sacred Sound

Let's start with sound. "In the beginning was the Word," the Gospel of St. John tells us. The idea that sound is primal—the first cause out of which the universe arose—is the creation myth of many cultures. In *The Music of Life* the Sufi master Hazrat Inayat Khan writes, "The knower of the mystery of sound knows the mystery of the whole universe."

The *Upanishads* refer to God as "Nada Brahma"—the divine sound that animates the universe. *Nada* yoga—the mystical use of sound—originated in India thousands of years ago.

Listening to sound with focused awareness can be a meditation in itself. There are stories of Buddhist monks reaching enlightenment by sitting next to a waterfall until they became one with the roar of the water. The Baal Shem Tov, the father of Hasidism, "urged his students to direct their awareness equally to prayer, birdsong, rain, or a shout in the street," notes his descendant, author Perle Besserman, in *The Shambhala Guide to Kabbalah and Jewish Mysticism.* They learned, she explains, "to hear the voice of God in everything."

Chant

Like prayer, chant—singing or reciting sacred words, phrases, and verses—is a widespread form of spiritual practice, found in nearly every culture. Some chants and songs contain ancient teachings that were transmitted orally, long before written texts were made. In places like India, where chanting is second nature, devotees may spend hours on end repeating a sacred name or phrase—often while they go about their everyday tasks.

A chant can be as simple as a syllable or as complex as a chorale. The text can be a *mantra* or a poem or a passage of scripture. The tune can be a single note or a song or a *raga*—a classical Indian composition. What is common to all chants is that they are borne on the voice, the most basic musical instrument.

In the East chanting has been an integral part of Vedic, Hindu, and Buddhist practice. Tribal peoples all over the world have always chanted, often accompanied by sticks or drums. In the West there is a newer but no less vital tradition of chanting. Think of Gregorian chant, or Jewish prayer, or Vespers mass. In recent years recordings of cloistered monks and nuns have even topped the music charts.

But whether for worship or entertainment we Westerners are less likely to chant than our counterparts elsewhere in the world. Jill Purce, a British chanting expert who leads Healing Voice workshops, thinks our failure to make sacred sound together is one reason for our culture's widespread disaffection. Her mission, she likes to say, is to "reenchant the world."

- *Mantra:* From Sanskrit word *manas* ("mind") and *trai* ("protect" or "free from"), a syllable or syllables repeated or chanted as a tool to free the mind.

- *Sutra:* Sanskrit for "thread," in Hinduism it is a verse or aphorism used to convey a teaching; in Buddhism, it is a teaching talk by the Buddha.

- *Dharani:* Short sutra, or teaching verse, that is chanted.

- *Gatha:* A song embedded in a sutra.

Purce was one of the first Westerners to study with the chantmaster of the Gyuto Tantric College (home of a now-famous choir of Tibetan monks who have inspired musicians such as John Cage and Philip Glass) and with a Mongolian master. Since then she has introduced thousands of Americans and Europeans to the exotic sounds of overtone chanting. Overtone chanting varies from culture to culture, but the principle remains the same: one note is sounded by the voice, then by reshaping the mouth and tongue, tones of higher frequency (overtones) are produced simultaneously, so that a single voice emits what sounds like a chord. (Huston Smith, the renowned expert on world religions, calls the technique "one-voice chording.") Tibetan chanting rests on uncommonly deep bass notes; Mongolian chanting is higher, with overtones that resemble the sound made by running a wet finger around the rim of a crystal glass. Producing—or even just listening to—these tones induces "a state of extreme calm and clarity," Purce says.

Overtone chanting is complicated to master, but learning the basics is easier than we think, according to musician and author Don Campbell, founder of the Institute for Music, Health, and Education in Boulder, Colorado. Campbell, who coined the term *The Mozart Effect* to describe music's ability to enhance learning, creativity, and health, points out that we create overtones in ordinary speech, whenever we pronounce vowels (see "Making Overtones," page 136).

Sound is a powerful means of promoting spiritual development, the doorway to soul in every culture. In *The Roar of Silence* Don Campbell notes:

> *The mystery schools of sound knew the vital importance of the connection between spirit and body. They used patterns of tone, movement, and breath to open the inner gates where awakened energy could flow between the subconscious and conscious worlds. The awakening of these inner and outer worlds does not come from overstimulation. It is not a frantic realization. It is a burst in seeing, listening, and feeling every part of life in harmony and balance.*

The effects of overtone chanting are dramatic, but other types of chanting are also powerful. Research shows that sound is vibrational medicine: it stimulates the immune system, triggers the release of endorphins—natural painkillers—regulates heart rate, improves memory and coordination, and induces relaxation. And those are just the physiological benefits. In *Chanting* musician Robert Gass, founder of the choral group

On Wings of Song and the recording company Spring Hill Music, suggests a few of the reasons we chant:

> *We chant to join our voices to the voices of countless seekers, worshipers, mystics, and lovers of life, in every time and in every place, who have shared in sacred song. We chant to fill our hearts and fill our homes with loving and peaceful vibrations of sound. We chant because it's fun.*

Gass calls chant "vocal meditation" and "singing our prayers." The best part of all is that it doesn't matter if your third-grade teacher said you were tone deaf; you don't need to be able to hold a tune to chant. (Gregorian Chant is sung in unison, but Zen Buddhist chanting is notably cacophonous!)

Toning

Toning—vocalizing with extended vowel sounds—is the simplest form of chant. Each vowel sound emits a different vibration, which can alter cell chemistry and lead to physical healing and emotional release, as well as to heightened states of awareness. The overall result of toning is to bring body, mind, and spirit into harmony. Robert Gass encourages us to let go and let ourselves "play" in order to get the hang of it. "Think of yourself as an explorer," he suggests in *Chanting.* "Your ship is your voice, and you will use it to journey into strange new worlds." To begin the journey, try the exercise Gass suggests in "Toning," below.

Try This: Toning

Now it's time to enjoy letting our voices play with the ancient practice of toning. . . . I will give you a basic map and some routes to try.

Take a vowel sound, for example: "Ohhhhh!" Stay with it for . . . four or five minutes. Experiment. Sing, "Ohhhhh," on a single note. See if you can make the tone vibrate in different parts of your body. Play with making subtle changes in the shape of your tongue, jaw, and lips while sustaining the tone. Sweep up and down your vocal range chanting, "Ohhhhh!" Try slow, elongated melodies with your vowel sound.

Now try the same with "Eeeeee." Then with "Ahhhhh." And with any other syllables you can choose . . . or invent.

Like a bold explorer, cast yourself into the unknown. Give yourself to the toning, and see where it takes you.

—ROBERT GASS, *CHANTING*

Mantra

Mantras are an integral part of Hindu, Tibetan Buddhist, Sufi, and Eastern Ortho-dox worship. A mantra—from the Sanskrit roots *manas* ("mind" or "consciousness") and *trai* ("protect" or "free from")—is a syllable, word, or phrase that evokes or cele-brates the divine, and is a vehicle for increasing spiritual awareness. As the mantra is repeated over and over, it clears the mind of ordinary thoughts and paves the way for reaching oneness with spirit.

Traditionally, a mantra is passed directly from teacher to student, as a tool for awakening. Mantras given in this way are thought to be endowed with special power that can hasten the student's unfolding, as well as heal the body-mind. In *Healing Mantras* author Thomas Ashley-Farrand points out some of the benefits of mantra practice—*japa* yoga, as it is known in the Hindu tradition:

> *Mantra can help you feel more peaceful or more energized. It can help you cope with illness, and it can sometimes help effect physical healing. It can help you deal with difficult or unpleasant cir-cumstances, by helping you see a course of action, or it can give you the patience and perspective just to "wait it out." It can help you bring your wishes to fruition and create reality from your dreams. Mantra is a dynamic, individual, nonviolent way to approach conditions you wish to change. [Mantras] are ancient formulas of divine sounds recorded by the ancient sages of India and held in trust and in secret for ages in both India and Tibet.*

Each mantra has a "seed" or *bija*—a specific sound frequency at which it vibrates—that gives it a singular effect. This seed plants itself in our minds and helps us become one with Greater Mind, according to Swami Sivananda Radha, a Western yoga teacher trained in India who headed an ashram in Canada. In chanting or reciting the mantra we gradually begin to resonate "with some other center of vibration vastly more powerful" than ourselves, Swami Radha explains in *Mantra: Words of Power.*

A mantra not only leads us to greater consciousness, it also protects us from our own negativity and obsessive thoughts. When we are anxious and upset, for example, repeating a mantra can change our state of mind altogether, points out Tibetan

Buddhist teacher Sogyal Rinpoche in *The Tibetan Book of Living and Dying* (see "Mantra," above).

Any syllables or words can become a mantra. In *Chanting,* Robert Gass tells a story about his eighty-year-old grandmother, who taught herself meditation out of a book and practiced it successfully for many years. When he asked what mantra she used, she told him that the book had said to pick an Indian word, so she had chosen *Cheyenne.* Using a Native American word rather than a Sanskrit one apparently hadn't hindered her practice one bit.

When Transcendental Meditation (TM) became popular in America in the 1970s, there were jokes that teachers were giving out words like *Coca-Cola* as mantras. But unless you worship the symbols of capitalism, you're better off picking a mantra that has an established sacred use. The British scientist Rupert Sheldrake cites compelling evidence that any repetitive behavior sets up a field of "morphic resonance," meaning that the more often an experience is repeated, the more likely it is the same results will occur in the future. By this thinking, a mantra that has proved beneficial over many centuries is more likely to produce a positive effect for you too.

Certain syllables or sounds are considered particularly auspicious. For Buddhists one such sound is AH. "AH is considered the source of all speech and sound—the sound of openness," explains Tibetan Buddhist scholar Tulku Thondup Rinpoche in *The Healing Power of Mind.* "The gentle chanting of this sound is a smooth, openhearted meditation." (For suggestions on how to meditate with AH, see "Soothing Through AH, the Sound of Openness," above).

Expressing Devotion

Chanting is a fundamental practice of devotional paths such as Sufism and bhakti yoga that center on a yearning for the divine. Many of the traditional chants are hymns to God in His or Her many guises. In notes for his album *One Track Heart,* the musician Krishna Das, an American who was for many years a disciple of the Hindu master Neem Karoli Baba, known as Maharaji, explains, "In this yoga, separateness is not seen as a roadblock on the path. It *is* the path. The devotee longs only to love more and more, to enjoy eternally the lover/Beloved relationship." As the chanting continues, the separation dissolves, and the lover—the disciple—becomes one with the Beloved—

God. A passage from the *Sivastotravali*, a classical poem to the Hindu deity Shiva, conveys a sense of the devotee's experience:

> *When everything in the world is in your form,*
> *How could there be a place*
> *Not suitable for devotees?*
> *Where in the word does their* mantra
> *Fail to bear fruit? . . .*

> *Lord! When the objective world has dissolved*
> *Through a state of deep meditation,*
> *You stand alone—*
> *And who does not see you then?*

Often, a mantra is a repetition of one of the thousands of names for God. "The name of God is greater than God," Krishna Das says, "because if you don't name God, you don't know where to look." In *Journey of Awakening*, Ram Dass (who, like Krishna Das, was a student of Maharaji) suggests repeating *Ram* (pronounced RAHM), a Sanskrit mantra short for "Rama." (The hero of the *Ramayana*, the oldest Hindu epic poem, Rama is an incarnation of Vishnu, the preserver aspect of the triune deity Brahma/Vishnu/Shiva—creator/protector/destroyer.) A longer version of this mantra is Sri Ram Ram Ram (SHREE RAHM RAHM RAHM). *Sri* means "venerable one."

Love is also the core of Sufism, often described as the mystical arm of Islam but in reality a path of devotion with broad influences ranging from Zoroastrianism to the teachings of Jesus. Repeating God's name is a core Sufi practice, called *dhikr* or *zikr*—literally "remembrance of God." "Through the practice of the *dhikr*," explains Llewellyn Vaughan-Lee in *Sufism: The Transformation of the Heart*, "the attention of the lover is turned toward God and the whole being of the lover becomes permeated with the joy of remembering the Beloved."

A Mantra Sampler

Here are some mantras that have been used by centuries of spiritual seekers. (For suggestions on how to work with a mantra, see "Mantra Practice," above.)

+ *Om* (OHM): The most famous mantra of all, this sacred Sanskrit syllable is the seed sound out of which the universe emerged, according to the *Upanishads*. Often the symbol for *Om* is visualized in the mind's eye as the mantra is chanted. *Om* is uttered on a single, attenuated note, with each nuance of the syllable melding into the next—a sound like "AhOhhhhhhhmmmmmm." *Om* is often combined with other words at the beginning and end of a prayer. One example is *Om Shanti* (OHM SHAHN-TEE). *Shanti* means "peace."

+ *Om Mani Padme Hum:* Another core mantra (pronounced OHM MA PEH-MEE HUNG in Tibetan), this means literally "the jewel in the lotus." The jewel represents the enlightened mind; the lotus is the heart of consciousness. This is the mantra associated with Chenrezig—the *Bodhisattva* of Compassion and patron deity of Tibet. The Dalai Lama is regarded as his incarnation.

The story goes that in deep meditation Chenrezig suddenly saw the depth of human suffering and vowed not to enter Nirvana (a state of everlasting enlightenment and the end of rebirth) until all suffering had been eliminated. This is the bodhisattva's vow, a central principle of Buddhism. A protector deity throughout Asia, Chenrezig is known as Avalokiteshvara in Sanskrit, Kwan Yin in Chinese, and Kannon or Kanzeon in Japanese.

✦ *Gate Gate Paragate, Parasamgate, Bodhi Svaha* (GAH-TAY GAH-TAY PAH-RAH-GAH-TAY, PAH-RAH-SAHM-GAH-TAY, BOH-DEE SVAH-HAH): This famous Sanskrit mantra is really a *gatha*—a chant or song contained in a *sutra* (a scripture), in this case the Heart Sutra, a key Buddhist teaching. This is the *gatha* that Chenresig/Avalokiteshvara was chanting when he experienced his awakening. Translations vary, but Ram Dass explains it as "Beyond, beyond, the Great Beyond, beyond that Beyond, to thee homage." *Beyond* in this instance means the vast unity we experience when we let go of ordinary dualistic thinking.

✦ *Om Ah Hum Vajra Guru Padma Siddhi Hum* (OHM AH HOOM VAJ-RAH GOO-ROO PAH-MAH HOOM; in Tibetan, OHM AH HUNG BEN-ZAH GOO-ROO PEH-MAH SID-DEE HUNG): This mantra is associated with Padmasambhava, who brought Buddhism to Tibet from India. It is the mantra of buddhas, spiritual masters, and other "realized beings," Sogyal Rinpoche explains. He particularly recommends it for peace, healing, and protection "in this violent, chaotic age."

✦ *Om Nama Shivaya* (OHM NAH-MAH SHEE-VAI-YAH): This is a well-known mantra asking Shiva—the destroyer aspect of the Hindu deity Brahma/Vishnu/Shiva—to remove our ignorance and other obstacles to spiritual realization.

✦ *Om Gum Gana Patayei Namaha* (OHM GUM GUH-NUH PUH-TUH YAY NAHM-AH-HAH): This is a Vedic and Hindu mantra for clearing away obstacles. In *Healing Mantras* Thomas Ashley-Farrand relates his experience using this mantra, with impressive results. He had been unable to find work for some time and hoped that this chant would help him get rid of whatever inner or outer barriers stood in his way. During forty days of continuous chanting Ashley-Farrand had a synchronistic encounter that led to a temporary job, then a permanent post that he kept for the next seven years.

+ *Hari Om* (HAH-REE OHM): This is a healing mantra, dedicated to Vishnu, the preserver aspect of the Hindu trinity. In Sanskrit *hari* means "dispeller of sins." This mantra calls for help in eliminating character flaws, which are thought to be the source of illness.

+ *La illaha illa 'llah hu* (LAH IL-AH-HAH IL-LAH LAH HOO): Translated from Arabic as "Nothing exists but Allah," or "There is only one God, Allah," this is a core mantra, or *wazifa*, of Sufism. In chanting these words "we lose our sense of identity and enter into the consciousness of the totality," The Sufi master Pir Vilayat explains in *The Call of the Dervish.* "This is what is meant by entering into the mind of God."

+ *Seed mantras:* Many single-syllable mantras are untranslatable, with no equivalent in language. Their meaning comes from the effect produced by the sound vibration—the seed sound. In *Healing Mantras* Thomas Ashley-Farrand gives instructions on working with several seed mantras, including *Shrim* (SHREEM). This sound, he says, generates the energy of abundance, represented by the Hindu goddess Lakshmi. Ancient teachings hold that if you repeat *Shrim* a hundred times, you will increase your prosperity a hundredfold.

+ *Life songs:* Physician Mitchell L. Gaynor, director of medical oncology and integrative medicine at the Strang-Cornell Cancer Prevention Center of New York Hospital, often recommends mantra meditation to facilitate healing and awareness. He suggests an exercise called "Life Songs" to help you connect with your inner essence. A life song, he explains in *Sounds of Healing,* is a mantralike string of three or four syllables arranged "in a pattern that is as unique to you as your social security number." To create your life song Dr. Gaynor recommends trying out different vowel-and-consonant combinations until you find the syllables that feel most harmonious to you. (Examples he gives include SOM MAN TUM and TA KEY LA.) "The goal," he says, "is to find a string of primal sounds that resonates within you as a profound expression of who you are."

- *Sacred words:* As in meditative prayer, discussed in Chapter 7, sacred words of any language can be used in mantra practice. Possibilities include *Ave Maria* (Latin for "Hail, Mary"), *Maranantha* (Aramaic for "Come, Lord"), *Kyrie* (ancient Greek for "Lord, have mercy"), and *Shalom* (Hebrew for "Peace"). You could also pick a word or phrase from any sacred text, such as the Bible, the *Tao Te Ching*, the *Bhagavad-Gita*, the *Upanishads*, or the *Dhammapada*.

- *Nature songs:* Remember those songs you learned around the campfire? Some of them are chants that we can sing as adults to express a deep connection with the cycles of nature and reverence for the Earth. One such chant is: "The earth, the air, the water, the fire. Return, return, return, return." Repeat as many times as you wish.

Chakra Mantras

In Hindu spiritual practice and mind-body healing much emphasis is placed on the *chakras*—the seven major energy centers of the body. One classic method of balancing and releasing the energy of the chakras consists of chanting the syllable associated with each chakra, beginning at the root chakra and proceeding upward through the body to the sixth chakra, or third eye. The seventh, or crown chakra, is thought to contain all sounds and is therefore not chanted in this exercise. The progression is as follows:

- Lam (LAHM): root chakra (base of the spine)
- Vam (VAHM): second chakra (genital area)
- Ram (RAHM): third chakra (solar plexus)
- Yam (YAHM): fourth chakra (heart)
- Hum (HOOM): fifth chakra (throat)
- Om (OHM): sixth chakra (third eye, between the eyebrows)

To work with these syllables effectively it is suggested that you sit in a comfortable but erect position, take a deep, relaxed breath through the nose, then, on a slow, even exhalation, sound the mantra for the first chakra. Inhale and repeat, moving on to the second syllable and second chakra. Continue through the entire progression, then begin again.

Learning to Chant

One of the easiest ways to start chanting is to sing along with an expert. There are many excellent recordings of individual teachers, groups, and spiritual communities performing chants (see "Resources"). You can, for example, accompany the Siddha yoga master Gurumayi Chidvilasananda as she chants "Om Nama Shivaya" at the tomb of her teacher, Swami Muktananda. Or sing *kirtan*—chanting in honor of God—with the musician Krishna Das. You can learn traditional Vedic and Hindu chants from the great Indian sitarist Ravi Shankar. Or chant the morning service with the *sangha*—spiritual community—of International Dai Bosatsu Zendo, an American Zen Buddhist temple. You can greet the dawn with Cherokee medicine woman Dhyani Ywahoo. Or repeat *Om* or *Kyrie* with British singer and voice teacher Chloë Goodchild.

Another way to learn chants is to find a spiritual center in your area that has periods devoted to chanting. Group chant is synergistic in its effect. Attuned to the rhythm of the chant, we literally begin to vibrate together at the same frequency. In a matter of minutes feelings of isolation, as well as tension and conflict, can melt away.

Healing Sound

The healing power of chant is by now widely recognized. Alfred Tomatis, a French doctor regarded as the father of sound healing, has called Gregorian chant "fabulous energy food." Just how nourishing it can be is revealed in the following tale. The time was the late 1960s, and the monks in a Benedictine monastery in France had fallen ill with inexplicable exhaustion. After several consultants failed to diagnose the problem, Tomatis was called in. He soon discovered that in a fit of reform following Vatican II, the abbot had abolished the monastery's traditional practice of singing Gregorian chants for several hours a day. Tomatis concluded that chant had been stimulating the monks' energy fields and—literally—keeping their bodies tuned physiologically. Without the practice they were wasting away. Within six months of resuming their chanting the monks were fully recovered and living happily on just a few hours of sleep a night.

Sound without voice—particularly that generated by sacred instruments such as drums, bells, gongs, singing bowls, sitars, horns, and harps—can also have a powerful effect on body, mind, and spirit. Think of the percussion-induced ecstatic states of African drummers and South American and Asian shamans. Or the transported expressions on the face of the dying as they are ushered across the threshold by Therese Schroeder-Sheker's harp. (A musician, she founded the Chalice of Repose project, a hospice palliative-care program based on what Schroeder-Sheker terms "music thanatology." It is headquartered at St. Patrick Hospital in Missoula, Montana.)

Mitchell Gaynor uses sound therapy extensively in his medical practice, especially techniques involving Tibetan singing bowls. An ancient vehicle for healing and spiritual awakening, the bowls—traditionally made of metal and now, often, of quartz crystal—emit harmonic overtones when a wooden baton is rubbed around the rim. "You can feel the vibrations resonating throughout your body," Dr. Gaynor explains in *Sounds of Healing,* "and when you stop, as the sound gradually dies away, you are likely to feel a lightness, a relief of pressure, in your head and body." Unlike drugs or other artificial "highs," sound produces a healthy and enduring lift, he says. "What we feel when we play a singing bowl is the real thing—a moment out of time that offers a release from the distractions and stresses of the outside world."

Songs of Devotion

Like chant, song and mystical poetry are vehicles for bringing us closer to the divine. Over the millennia devotees in all walks of life—from poets to scholars to kings—

have poured their love and longing for God into hymns and verse. Their words reverberate with the agony and ecstasy of the spiritual quest.

The 150 songs and poems that make up the Old Testament Book of Psalms, many of them the work of the great King David, include hymns of thanksgiving and praise, laments by those who feel abandoned by the Lord or estranged from him, and petitions for God's help. The words of Psalm 100, "Make a joyful noise unto the Lord, all ye lands," are a straightforward expression of the importance of song in worship since ancient times. "Serve the Lord with gladness," Psalm 100 exhorts. "Come before His presence with singing."

The Song of Solomon, or Song of Songs, is one of the most famous Biblical love poems to God. Attributed to King Solomon, son of David and Bathsheba, it is known for its erotic imagery, the Old Testament's most stirring hymn to the Beloved.

But it is from the perfumed gardens of the ancient East that we get some of the most evocative verses ever written to God. They are the work of Indian poet-saints such as Kabir and Mirabai, and Sufi philosophers and poets such as Hafiz and Jalaluddin Rumi, a thirteenth-century mystic and scholar who is the best-selling poet in America today. Rumi's passionate outpourings to the Beloved virtually define the nature of the devotional spiritual path—from the first whispers of the call, through the bliss of loving and the wrenching surrender of the ego, to the joy and harmony of

Inspiration: A Mine of Rubies

Last night I learned how to be a lover of God,
To live in this world and call nothing my own.

. . .

Within the cavern of my soul
I heard the voice of a lover crying,
"Drink now! Drink now!"—
I took a sip and saw the vast ocean—
Wave upon wave caressed my soul.

—JALALUDDIN RUMI, "A MINE OF RUBIES"

living in union with God (see "Mine of Rubies," page 148). Who could resist a spiritual invitation such as this one, written by Rumi?

Come, come whoever you are—
Wanderer, worshiper, lover of leaving—
What does it matter?
Ours is not a caravan of despair.
Come, even if you have broken your vows
A hundred times—
Come, come again, come.

The message of Sufism is not to run off to a monk's cell or mountaintop to praise God in solitude. To the Sufis the contemplative life means embracing the Beloved fully—right here, right now. As the mystic and poet Andrew Harvey explains in *Perfume of the Desert,* the Sufis are instruments of the sacred in the everyday world:

Wherever they are, a light of God is; whatever they do, God does in them; their words inspire divine love and their actions radiate the clarity of divine justice and the generosity of divine mercy. What is remarkable about those who reach this glory is that they are always humble and integrated.

Every spiritual path leads inward, to union with sacred source. The Sufi path, as Llewellyn Vaughan-Lee notes in *Sufism: The Transformation of the Heart,* "is suited to those who need to realize their relationship with God as a love affair, who need to be drawn by the thread of love and longing back to their Beloved." Lifting our voices in words and song is a way of hastening our surrender on the devotional path.

Sacred Vision

Just as sound can lead us to a closer connection to the sacred, so can sight. Objects of contemplation run the gamut from the chakras—often visualized as "wheels of light" or lotus flowers opening to signify spiritual unfolding—to a concrete image of a deity or some other representation of the divine. A visual meditation can be as straightforward as gazing at a candle, or a flower, or the stars, or a beautiful vista. Or it can be as elaborate as mentally constructing a Tibetan Buddhist mandala or the Kabbalist Tree of Life, with all the colors, names, sounds, qualities, and meditations associated with the ten *sefirot*—or attributes of God—that make up its branches. In every case the object of contemplation is intended to evoke an inner experience of the divine.

Visualization is an ancient spiritual and healing practice. "In Tibetan Buddhism we regularly use visualization techniques to help us connect with a more sacred reality," Lama Surya Das explains in *Awakening to the Sacred.* "We might, for example, visualize ourselves in a Buddha-field of luminous light."

Tulku Thondup urges us to "be creative in imagining light" in our meditations. In *The Healing Power of Mind* he suggests ways to call up light for healing our bodies and emotions (see "Visualizing Light," below).

Light also figures in mystical Jewish practice. One meditation from the *Zohar*, a Kabbalistic text, involves contemplating a flame until one becomes aware of all five colors contained in it—white, yellow, red, black, and sky blue (see "Contemplating a Flame," page 151). As Aryeh Kaplan explains in *Jewish Meditation*, white, yellow, and red refer to the colors of the flame; black, to the darkness surrounding it. Blue, according

Try This: Visualizing Light

You might find it helpful to imagine light showering down upon you, suffusing and radiating your mind and body with its healing warmth, bringing openness and relaxation to everything it touches. Or you might imagine light coming from your source of power. Perhaps the light takes the form of rainbow-colored beams. Feel that it is filling your mind and body completely, bringing bliss, peace, and health that instantly warms and heals problem areas, or melts them into light and peace. Every part of your body, down to the last cell, is effortlessly filled with light. Then feel that your body is transformed into a body of light, or perhaps a glowing, warm flame if that image is helpful.

—TULKU THONDUP RINPOCHE, *THE HEALING POWER OF MIND*

to the Zohar, represents the Divine Presence. It is the color of the aura—*tzelem* in Hebrew—the energy field around objects. As you become more adept at contemplation, the ability to see auras increases.

Yantras and Mandalas

Many traditions—particularly Tibetan Buddhism, Hinduism, Native American spirituality, and Eastern Orthodox Christianity—use specific figures as objects of concentration or memory aids for visualization. *Yantras* and *mandalas*—mystical diagrams—are Tantric meditation devices. Tantra yoga involves awakening *kundalini*—the powerful spiritual energy that lies latent at the base of the spine—to reach union with the divine. Sensory stimuli are neither ignored nor transcended but become the basis of spiritual practice.

A yantra is the visual equivalent of a mantra: like a mantra, it is believed to embody sacred energy. The pattern of a yantra contains geometric figures—squares, diamonds, circles, and, sometimes, lotus-leaf shapes—within a square surround. Each of the elements has specific symbolism: a downward-pointing triangle, for example, represents the masculine principle; an upward-pointing one, the feminine. The midpoint, or seed, of the yantra signifies the creative principle of the universe. In contemplating the figure the meditator eventually reaches a transcendent state.

A mandala—"sacred circle" in Sanskrit—also symbolizes union with the divine. Like the yantra's midpoint its center is the place of spiritual illumination. The artist and educator Judith Cornell notes in *Mandala:*

> *The Navajo call this center "a spiritual place of emergence" for sacred imagery. By focusing on it both mandala artist and meditator can open to the divine energies of the deities and to the contents of his or her own spiritual and psychological self.*

The mandala used in Tibetan Buddhist practice is, in effect, a two-dimensional shrine. The square surround symbolizes the "temple" and the four sides, or "doors," represent the four directions—North, South, East, and West. The various elements within the mandala call up different cosmic forces. (The four directions are central elements in another kind of mandala, the medicine wheel, which is integral to the spiritual practice of tribal cultures in North America. See "Teachings of the Medicine Wheel," below.)

Inspiration: Teachings of the Medicine Wheel

Like the mandala the Native American medicine wheel is oriented to the four directions. The medicine wheel represents the universe, the whole, the mirror in which everything is reflected, the Way. According to the Native American writer Hyemeyohsts Storm, north is the seat of wisdom, symbolized by the power animal the Buffalo and the color white. South is the place of innocence and trust. Its "medicine color" is green; its animal, the mouse. East, symbolized by the eagle and the color yellow, is the place of illumination, "where we can see things clearly and wide." West is the place of introspection; its color is black; its totem, the bear. At birth each of us is given a particular starting place on the wheel: that perspective will be our most natural way of perceiving the world throughout our lives. But sticking to your original gift will make you a "partial" person, according to Storm. We "must grow by seeking understanding in each of the four great ways," he emphasizes in *Seven Arrows*.

A mandala may be the centerpiece of a *thangka,* a Tibetan Buddhist scroll painting framed in silk. *Thangkas* are often constructed around the image of a key spiritual figure, such as Manjushri, the *Bodhisattva* of Wisdom, or Tara, the feminine aspect of compassion, or one of the many manifestations of Buddha. The image is used for "taking refuge"—showing reverence for or, in effect, merging with the deity.

In the Eastern Orthodox Church *ikons*—religious pictures or statues, usually of Christ or Mary—are used as devotional objects. Byzantine and Medieval art was sacred in intention, expressing the devotion of the artist and helping the worshiper unite with God. Stained-glass windows also serve this function, depicting individuals or scenes that direct our attention to the divine.

The author and mystic Andrew Harvey tells a poignant story that illustrates the force of sacred imagery. At the end of an intense and moving week at the bedside of his dying father, Harvey went to the Sunday service at the Catholic church he had attended as a boy growing up in India. At one point he looked up at a statue of Jesus on the cross, and suddenly, he recalls,

The cross actually came alive for about fifteen or twenty minutes, and I knew that Jesus was sending me waves of unconditional love. I had never experienced anything remotely like it. For the first time I began to glimpse what the sacrifice on the cross means inside the heart. It's a total embrace of all the terms of life, all the ordeals. After the service was over I went outside, and there in the dust outside the gate was this helpless young man with no arms and no legs. I heard a voice within me say that I must devote the rest of my life to serving the abandoned, the poor, and the maimed. The real importance of having a mystical awakening is not to revel in it but to devote yourself totally to transforming the conditions that caused the agony and terror that are destroying the world today.

RESOURCES

BOOKS

Ashley-Farrand, Thomas. *Healing Mantras.* New York: Ballantine Wellspring, 1999.

Barks, Coleman, trans., and others. *The Essential Rumi.* San Francisco: Harper San Francisco, 1997.

Beaulieu, John. *Music and Sound in the Healing Arts.* Berkeley: Station Hill Press, 1987.

Berendt, Joachim-Ernst. *The World Is Sound: Nada Brahma.* Rochester, Vt.: Destiny Books, 1987.

Besserman, Perle. *The Shambhala Guide to Kabbalah and Jewish Mysticism.* Boston: Shambhala, 1997.

The Song of God: Bhagavad-Gita. New York: New American Library, 1993.

Campbell, Don G. *The Mozart Effect.* New York: Avon, 1997.

———. *The Roar of Silence.* Wheaton, Ill.: The Theosophical Publishing House, 1989.

Cornell, Judith, PhD. *Mandala.* Wheaton, Ill.: Quest, 1994.

Das, Lama Surya. *Awakening to the Sacred.* New York: Broadway, 1999.

Dass, Ram. *Journey of Awakening.* New York: Bantam, 1978.

The Dhammapada. P. Lal, trans. New York: Farrar, Straus & Giroux, 1967.

Gardner-Gordon, Joy. *The Healing Voice.* Freedom, Cal.: The Crossing Press, 1993.

Gass, Robert, with Kathleen Brehony. *Chanting.* New York: Broadway, 1999.

Gaynor, Mitchell, M.D. *Sounds of Healing.* New York: Broadway, 1999.

Harvey, Andrew, and Eryk Hanut. *Perfume of the Desert.* Wheaton, Ill.: Quest, 1999.

How to Know God: The Yoga Aphorisms of Patanjali. New York: New American Library, 1953.

Hull, Arthur. *Drum Circle Spirit.* Sacramento: White Cliffs Media, 1998 (with CD).

Kaplan, Aryeh. *Jewish Meditation.* New York: Schocken, 1985.

Khan, Hazrat Inayat. *The Inner Life.* Boston: Shambhala, 1997.

———. *The Music of Life.* Indianapolis: Omega Publications, 1983.

Khan, Pir Vilayat Inayat. *The Call of the Dervish.* Indianapolis: Omega Publications, 1981.

Lao-Tzu. *Tao Te Ching.* Stephen Mitchell, trans. New York: Harper & Row, 1988.

Le Mée, Katharine. *Chant.* New York: Bell Tower, 1994.

Marshall, Henry. *Mantras.* Woodside, Cal.: Bluestar, 1999 (with CD).

Olatunji, Babatunde. *Drums of Passion Songbook.* Brooklyn: Olatunji Music, 1993.

Purce, Jill. *The Mystic Spiral: Journey of the Soul.* New York: Thames & Hudson, 1980.

Radha, Swami Sivananda. *Mantras: Words of Power.* Delhi, India: Motilal Banarsidass, 1980.

Redmond, Layne. *When the Drummers Were Women.* New York: Three Rivers, 1997.

Simpkinson, Anne A., and Charles H. Simpkinson. *Soul Work.* New York: Harper-Perennial, 1998.

Sogyal Rinpoche. *The Tibetan Book of Living and Dying.* San Francisco: Harper San Francisco, 1992.

Storm, Hyemeyohsts. *Seven Arrows.* New York: Ballantine, 1972.

Thondup, Tulku. *The Healing Power of Mind.* Boston: Shambhala, 1996.

Tomatis, Alfred A. *The Conscious Ear.* Berkeley: Station Hill Press, 1991.

The Upanishads. New York: New American Library, 1990.

Vaughan-Lee, Llewellyn. *Sufism: The Transformation of the Heart.* Inverness, Cal.: The Golden Sufi Center, 1995.

PERIODICALS

Hinduism Today
Himalayan Academy
107 Kaholalele Road
Kapaa, HI 96746
(808) 822–7032

Shamanism Magazine
c/o Foundation for Shamanic Studies
PO Box 1939
Mill Valley, CA 94942
(415) 380–8282

Shaman's Drum: A Journal of Experiential Shamanism
3600A Cedar Flat Road
Williams, OR 97544
(541) 846–1313
sdrm@mind.net

Sufi Review
Pir Publications
227 West Broadway
New York, NY 10013
(212) 334–5212

Sufism
PO Box 2382
San Rafael, CA 94912
ias@ias.org

VIDEO/AUDIO

Chalice of Repose. Therese Schroeder-Sheker. A contemplative musician's approach to death and dying (Sounds True) VHS.

Chant. The Benedictine Monks of Santo Domingo de Silos. Pop-chart-topping Gregorian chant (Angel).

Chant: Spirit in Sound. Robert Gass and On Wings of Song. Chants from all over the world (Spring Hill).

Chants of India. Ravi Shankar. Classical mantras from the *Vedas, Upanishads,* and other scriptures, set to music by the noted sitarist and composer (Angel).

Devi. Chloë Goodchild. Devotional chants from Hindu, Buddhist, Christian, and Sufi traditions (The Naked Voice, distributed by Raven).

Divine Singing. Chaitanya Kabir. How to chant in the Indian devotional tradition (Sounds True).

Drums of Passion. Babatunde Olatunji. Nigerian drummer who influenced John Coltrane, Carlos Santana, and Mickey Hart (Columbia).

Freedom Chants from the Roof of the World. The Gyuto Monks. Traditional chants performed by the Tibetan Buddhist monks of the Gyuto Tantric College in India (Rykodisc).

Mantra. Thomas Ashley-Farrand. Over eight hours of instruction on using sacred words of power (Sounds True).

Mantras for Releasing Fear. Shri Anandi Ma and Dileepji Pathak. Chanting of mantras to calm the emotions and restore inner balance (Sounds True).

Music for The Mozart Effect. Don Campbell. Music for healing the body, strengthening the mind, and releasing the creative spirit (Spring Hill).

Nada Yoga. Russell Paul. Experiencing the ancient science of sound (Healing Music).

Om Namaha Shivaya. Robert Gass and On Wings of Song. Discovering deep relaxation and inner peace with a well-known mantra (Spring Hill).

One Track Heart and *Pilgrim Heart.* Krishna Das. Devotional chants and songs (Triloka).

Overtone Chanting. Jill Purce. Powerful, meditative tape with solo and group Mongolian overtone chanting (Inner Sound, see ORGANIZATIONS).

The Power of the Mantra. Siddha yoga master Gurumayi Chidvilasananda chanting Om Namah Shivaya at Baba Muktananda's shrine in Ganeshpuri, India (SYDA Foundation).

The Power of Mantras. Swami Sivananda Radha. Traditional mantras explained and chanted by a Western Hindu master (Timeless Books).

The Power of Mantras. Thomas Ashley-Farrand. Using sacred words for protection, abundance, creativity, and healing (Sounds True).

Prayer. Multicultural prayers and chants by His Holiness the Dalai Lama, Jai Uttal, Rebbe Soul, Krishna Prema Das, and others (Soundings of the Planet).

Rhythms of the Chakras. Glen Velez. Drumming for the body's energy centers (Sounds True).

Rivers of One. Oruc Guvenc and Tumata. Traditional Sufi music (1998).

Shakuhachi Meditation Music. Stan Richardson. Bamboo flute for contemplation (Sounds True).

Shiva Station. Jai Uttal and the Pagan Love Orchestra. Devotional music (Triloka).

Song of the Sun. Andrew Harvey. The life, poetry, and teachings of Rumi (Sounds True).

Sound Healing. Dean Evenson and Soundings Ensemble. Music for meditation and relaxation (Soundings of the Planet).

The Sound of Zen in America. Chanting at International Dai Bosatsu Zendo, a monastery in New York State's Catskill Mountains (The Zen Studies Society, 223 East Sixty-seventh St., New York, NY 10021).

Sunsongs. Ven. Dhyani Ywahoo. Native American chants (Sunray Meditation Society, PO Box 308, Bristol, VT 05443).

Trance 1. Sufi dervish rite, Tibetan overtone chanting, and *dhrupad,* Indian classical music (Ellipsis Art).

Trance 2. Sufi *zikr,* Moroccan healing rite, and Balinese temple music (Ellipsis Art).

World Music That Speaks to the Spirit. Chants and songs by Jai Uttal, Krishna Das, Ali Akbar Khan, Wasis Diop, and others (Triloka).

Yoga Zone Music for Meditation. Music to create inner peace by Ravi Shankar, Will Ackerman, Tim Story, and others (Windham Hill).

ORGANIZATIONS
Abode of the Message
5 Abode Road
New Lebanon, NY 12125
(518) 794–8095

The Chalice of Repose Project
at St. Patrick Hospital
(Therese Schroeder-Sheker)
School of Music-Thanatology
554 W. Broadway
Missoula, MT 59802
(406) 329–2810

Don Campbell, Inc.
PO Box 4179
Boulder, CO 80306
(303) 440–8046

The Healing Voice (Jill Purce)
c/o Inner Sound
246 Colney Hatch Lane
London N10 1BD
(011) 44181 444–4855

International Dai Bosatsu Zendo
HCR 1, Box 171
Livingston Manor, NY 12758
(914) 439–4566

Kripalu Center for Yoga and Health
Box 793, West Street
Lenox, MA 02140
(800) 967–3577

The Naked Voice
(Chloë Goodchild)
PO Box 1892
Bath BA3 6xx, England
(011) 44–8700–768769
info@nvoice.globalnet.co.uk

Satchidananda Ashram-Yogaville
Route I, Box 1720
Buckingham, VA 23921
(804) 969–3121

Tibet House
22 West Fifteenth Street
New York, NY 10011
(212) 807–0563

WEB SITES

www.cloudnet.com/~abartell/SilverIconCatWebSites.html
Religious Icons of the World Wide Web, with gallery of Peter Pearson's Christian
iconic images and information on his workshops, retreats, and icon-painting kits.

www.drumcircle.com
Site for the drumming community, set up by Arthur Hull, father of the drum circle
movement.

www.jillpurce.com
Information on Jill Purce and The Healing Voice, with workshop schedule and tapes
to order.

www.sanskritmantra.com
Author Thomas Ashley-Farrand on Hindu and Buddhist mantras and mantra-based
spiritual disciplines.

www.shamanism.org
Site of Foundation for Shamanic Studies, with information on workshops and trainings, and list of certified Harner Method Shamanic Counselors.

www.sufism.org/threshld
Educational foundation of the Mevlevi (dervish) Sufi order, which offers trainings
and seminars around the world.

9.

Moving

with Spirit

Dance, my heart! Dance today with joy.

—KABIR

Can't sit still? Prefer movement to words? Don't worry. That won't keep you off the contemplative path. In fact, some of history's most devout mystics have moved and shaken their way to God. The mystery schools of the East included music and movement in their menu of sacred practices. The great cathedrals of the Middle Ages rocked with song and dance in praise of the divine—a tradition of celebration that maverick theologians like Matthew Fox are reviving today. And seekers in every culture continue the age-old, spirit-renewing ritual of pilgrimage. If you can walk, you can meditate. If you can dance, you can pray. Anyone, no matter how restless or rebellious, can find a way to connect with the divine.

Body and Spirit

The body has been in and out of favor in spiritual circles since ancient times. Thousands of years ago, the goddess religions worshiped the body for its fecundity, like the earth's. The early Greeks celebrated the body as a temple for spirit. But by the fourth century B.C., the Greeks had come to regard the body as an impediment to spiritual ascent, a prison for the soul. Over the centuries since, Christian contemplatives have sought God through self-denial and self-control—"mortification of the flesh" aimed at eliminating whatever stands in the way of direct spiritual experience. If you've ever been in an altered state from exhaustion, you know that when the discursive mind is stilled even momentarily, what William Blake called "the doors of perception" swing open to another level of reality, a feeling of mystical union. Like the Desert Fathers and Mothers—many of them hermits—ascetics in every tradition have used fasting, isolation, and sleep deprivation as paths to higher awareness.

In the East there is a long tradition of Hindu holy men wandering homeless, with no other possessions than their loincloths, in an effort to transcend the limitations of the flesh. Gautama Siddhartha (later known as the Buddha—the Awakened One) went through a period of asceticism before settling on the more moderate road to enlightenment he called "the Middle Way." Rigorous fasting and other abstinent behavior may indeed induce states of ecstasy and heightened awareness. And the occasional sensible (and supervised) fast is an excellent way to purify body and mind. But extreme denial of the body isn't necessary for spiritual awakening, nor is it the best course for most of us who live and work in the everyday world.

The body is, in fact, the vehicle for spiritual life, and, as such, it deserves nurturing and care. The writer Dan Wakefield, in *How Do We Know When It's God?*, asserts that in spiritual matters, words can fail or mislead us, but the body never lies:

> *The body isn't fooled. When it starts to protest, resisting our intentions and actions through headaches, trembling, nausea—any and all of the signs of anxiety and disturbance—we had better pay attention. Does it react this way whenever [a] new course is thought about or planned or advanced? Stop, look, and listen. Don't just listen to the words of others; listen to the message*

of your own being. Pay attention. The poet Mary Oliver says, "I don't know how to pray, but I know how to pay attention." That's the deepest kind of prayer.

When you sit down to meditate or pray, one of the first things you notice is the state of your body: Is it warm or cold? Stiff or supple? Comfortable or in pain? As David Yount points out in *Breaking Through God's Silence,*

We pray with our bodies as well as our spirits. Just as we dress our bodies to suit life's occasions, we use them in prayer to express our attitude. . . . In Christianity the tradition of standing for prayer is ancient; kneeling is more recent. At one time monks prayed with arms outstretched, denoting both their openness to God and the posture of Jesus on the cross.

It is not just in prayer that we use our bodies to express reverence, humility, gratitude, or devotion—to "carry" us to spirit. Moving meditations are an integral part of many traditions, from *kinhin,* the walking meditation of Zen Buddhists, to tracing the path of the labyrinth—a practice with a long ecumenical history—to the whirling of Sufi dervishes and the freeform, nondenominational ebullience of ecstatic dance. Hatha yoga and many of the martial arts focus on developing the body as the path to sacred union.

"Enlightenment," points out Georg Feuerstein in *The Yoga Tradition,* "is a whole-body event."

Walking

Let's begin with the most natural form of movement for most of us—walking. Slow, deliberate walking is a time-honored form of Buddhist practice. "People usually consider walking on water or in thin air a miracle," the Vietnamese Zen monk Thich Nhat Hanh tells us in *The Miracle of Mindfulness.* "But I think the real miracle is . . . to walk on earth." Thich Nhat Hanh is known for leading silent walks wherever he is—whether in the countryside around his French retreat center, Plum Village, or in the heart of

Try This: Walking Meditation

Walking meditation can be very enjoyable. We walk slowly, alone or with friends, if possible in some beautiful place. Walking meditation is really to enjoy the walking—walking not in order to arrive, just for walking. The purpose is to be in the present moment and enjoy each step you make. Therefore you have to shake off all worries and anxieties, not thinking of the future, not thinking of the past, just enjoying the present moment. . . . We walk all the time, but usually it is more like running. . . . Our mind darts from one thing to another, like a monkey swinging from branch to branch without stopping to rest. Thoughts have millions of pathways, and we are forever pulled along them into the world of forgetfulness. If we can transform our walking path into a field for meditation, our feet will take every step in full awareness. Our breathing will be in harmony with our steps, and our mind will naturally be at ease. Every step we take will reinforce our peace and joy and cause a stream of calm energy to flow through us. Then we can say, "With each step, a gentle wind blows."

—THICH NHAT HANH, *PRESENT MOMENT, WONDERFUL MOMENT*

New York City. Any moment can be a meditative moment, Thich Nhat Hanh teaches us. "Peace," he is fond of saying, "is every step." Try his suggestions for mindful walking ("Walking Meditation," above).

Kinhin is walking zazen. In a *zendo*—Zen Buddhist practice hall—periods of sitting meditation are generally interspersed with *kinhin*. "You are to think of this walking as zazen in motion," the great Japanese master Yasutani Roshi tells us in *The Three Pillars of Zen*, edited by his student Philip Kapleau Roshi. The instructions are simple but precise (see "Kinhin," page 164). "Walk calmly and steadily, with poise and dignity," Yasutani Roshi exhorts. "The mind must be kept taut. . . ."

Insight meditation—also known as *Vipassana*—has its own method of walking practice. Each step is even slower and more deliberate than in *kinhin*. Sometimes the movement is almost imperceptible. Pick an unobstructed path ten to twenty steps long, then walk back and forth mindfully. One way to practice walking meditation is to combine it with "noting"—closely attending to every aspect of your movement.

Each time you pick up and place a foot, mentally repeat, *lifting, moving, placing.* Plant one foot fully and firmly before lifting the other. Whenever your mind wanders—as it invariably will—gently bring it back to the sensation in your feet.

The Labyrinth

There is an exquisite form of walking meditation that involves following a labyrinth, or sacred path. This practice has become increasingly popular in recent years, as labyrinths have sprung up around the world, many painted on giant canvases that can be rolled out wherever there is a large, flat surface.

A labyrinth is a kind of mandala, a ritual path in the round. Although the labyrinth exists in many cultures, the first known appearance was in ancient Crete. According to Greek mythology the labyrinth was built for King Minos of Crete to imprison the Minotaur, the monstrous bull-man borne by Minos's wife after her illicit affair with a sacred white bull.

The modern-day labyrinth, patterned on the design inlaid on the floor of Chartres

Cathedral in the twelfth century, is not a maze—it has no trick twists and turns, or blind alleys, and no intention to confine or confound. Laid out in the form of a giant circle surrounding seven or eleven concentric circles, the labyrinth is a path with switchbacks that leads the seeker from a point on the perimeter to the sacred space at the center, then back out to the starting point. This circuit represents a connection with the divinity at our own core, according to the Reverend Lauren Artress, author of *Walking a Sacred Path*. "The labyrinth," she explains, "is an archetype of wholeness, a sacred place that helps us discover the depths of our souls."

Credit for reviving the labyrinth as a tool for spiritual practice goes largely to Artress, a psychotherapist and Episcopal priest who is canon for special ministries at Grace Cathedral in San Francisco. She first encountered the figure while attending the Mystery School led by master teacher Jean Houston. Artress oversaw the installation of a thirty-five-foot labyrinth at Grace Cathedral (there are now three) and began giving workshops around the country on its use.

Walking the labyrinth requires no special skill and, unlike most forms of meditation, no specific posture, or breathing, or mantra. "The sheer act of walking a complicated path—which discharges energy—begins to focus the mind," Artress explains. "Walking the labyrinth is a body prayer."

Each of us walks the path in a different way, bringing our own "hopes, dreams, history, and longings of the soul" to the experience, Artress says. But based on her observations she offers a few guidelines for how to make the labyrinth a spiritual practice (see "Walking the Labyrinth," page 166). No matter how diverse the approaches the benefits are strikingly similar, Artress finds:

> *Walking the labyrinth clears the mind and gives insight into the spiritual journey. It urges action. It calms people in the throes of life transitions. It helps them see their lives in the context of a path, a pilgrimage. They realize that they are not human beings on a spiritual path but spiritual beings on a human path. To those of us who feel we have untapped gifts to offer, it stirs the creative fires within. To others who are in deep sorrow, the walk gives solace and peace.*

Testimonials to the power of the labyrinth come from people of all faiths—as well as those with no formal affiliation—and from all walks of life. The outdoor labyrinth at Grace Cathedral is used around the clock. There is a policeman on the night beat

Try This: Walking the Labyrinth

Everyone will approach the labyrinth in a different way, notes the Reverend Lauren Artress. She recommends reflecting briefly on where you are in your life before you start walking. "This will help you get your bearings," she says. Other approaches include:

Gracious Attention: This means letting go of all thoughts and allowing whatever emerges, whether that means tears or a feeling of peace or some other response.

Asking a Question: Alternatively, you can reflect on a question you have or a decision to make, exploring all its facets. As you walk, an answer may emerge.

Repetition: You can focus the mind by silently repeating a mantra or phrase.

Reading Scripture: You can read the Bible or other sacred texts while walking.

Praying: "The labyrinth is a sacred space where we can talk to God," Artress points out.

who often walks it on his midnight dinner break. Many people walk it in the morning on their way to work, and it is a regular stop on the tourist circuit. Letters pour in to Artress attesting to the labyrinth's effect on people's lives.

"To walk a sacred path is to know and trust that there is guidance on this planet," Artress writes. Even watching others walk the path is a form of meditation, she finds:

Based on the circle, the universal symbol for unity and wholeness, the labyrinth sparks the human imagination and introduces it to a kaleidoscopic patterning that builds a sense of relationship: one person to another, to another, to many people, to creation of the whole. It enlivens the intuitive part of our nature and stirs within the human heart the longing for connectedness and the remembrance of our purpose for living.

To Artress, walking the labyrinth recreates the three stages of the Western mystical path—purgation, illumination, union. In working our way from the entrance to the center we quiet down and release whatever is blocking our connection with spirit. (Early monastics traveled this path on their knees as an act of penitence, Artress points out.) The center represents illumination; it is a place for meditation and prayer leading to clarity. The return walk symbolizes union—integrating spiritual awareness into the fabric of our lives.

The labyrinth offers many lessons. Sharon Salzberg, an American Buddhist teacher, recalls her first experience of it. "The way the labyrinth is laid out, you progress closer and closer to the center, then just as you think you are about to arrive, the path sends you off in the exact opposite direction, all the way out to the edge." Our lives are often like that, Salzberg reflects. We may be on the verge of reaching a goal—spiritual or otherwise—when the way suddenly veers, plunging us into doubt and confusion. But if we have faith and press on, she says, we may find that what seemed like a detour turns out to be the most direct way home.

Pilgrimage

There is a custom among the Australian aboriginals to "go walkabout"—take a sacred journey, or pilgrimage, on foot. Walking the labyrinth is one form of pilgrimage, but nearly every culture offers its own version. Moslems traditionally make a pilgrimage—a *hadj*—to the holy city of Mecca. Christians journey to the Holy Sepulchre in Jerusalem or to shrines where the Virgin Mary or various saints are said to have miraculously appeared. Jews leave prayers for loved ones at the Wailing Wall in Jerusalem. Tibetan Buddhists and Hindus circle Mount Kailash, the holiest of the Himalayas. In *The Art of Pilgrimage* author Phil Cousineau describes many such journeys, including a thousand-year-old tradition of walking a circuit of eighty-eight shrines on the Japanese island of Shikoku.

"Travel practice" is what Cousineau calls such trips. You can make a pilgrimage anywhere, anytime. All it requires, he suggests, is "taking your soul for a stroll":

> Long walks, short walks, morning walks, evening walks—whatever form or length it takes. Walking is the best way to get out of your head. Recall the invocation of [philosopher] Søren Aabye Kierkegaard, who said, "Above all, do not lose your desire to walk: Every day I walk my-

self into a state of well-being and walk away from every illness; I have walked myself into my best thoughts." [German philosopher] Friedrich Nietzsche also remarked, "Never trust a thought that didn't come by walking."

British author Roger Housden regularly leads silent meditation walks in the Sahara Desert. The vast desolation reminds him, he writes in *Sacred Journeys in a Modern World,* that "beneath the ticktock of my hopes and fears, past and future, there [is] nothing much to speak of at all, simply a sense of clear and empty space, rather like the desert itself."

At its best travel is transformative, stripping away pretense and certainty, creating an opportunity for renewal. When we go walkabout, even if only along a windy beach or under the cherry trees in the local park, we not only connect with nature—we meet ourselves. And if we walk long enough and look deep enough, we will encounter the vast spaciousness that Housden and all mystics speak of—that moment when our feelings of separation from the cosmos dissolve.

The Spirit of Exercise

You've no doubt heard of runner's high. It's more than just a physiological phenomenon, a release of endorphins that lifts your mood. Long-distance running is how many people leave behind everyday worries and obsessive thinking, and get in touch with something outside themselves. Whether you call it "being in the zone" or "making a soul connection," the feeling is the same.

In Tibet there are monks known as *lung-gompas* who perform superhuman feats, running hundreds of miles at a stretch. How do they do it? Their motto is: "Aim for Alpha Centauri"—a faraway star—"and keep your eyes on your feet." Like any moving meditation, including swimming or cycling or any other form of repetitive physical activity, running is not only an excellent concentration practice but also a metaphor for living consciously. It asks you to take a long view—to set a distant and challenging goal—then bring your attention to the here and now, and experience each step, each moment, as fully and mindfully as possible.

One practice you can do when you're running—or walking, for that matter—is to tune your senses to your surroundings. Listen to the sounds in the environment; identify everything you hear. Focus on colors and images; be open to whatever you see without judging it good or bad, pretty or ugly. Tune in to smells—flowering shrubs or the sea air or fresh bread wafting from a bakery. Be aware of how the air feels on your skin—temperature, moisture, a soft breeze, the slap of a winter gale.

Hatha Yoga

Every month, it seems, there's a new yoga class opening up in the neighborhood, with a different way of teaching this ancient Indian practice. Some forms, like Bikhram yoga, Jivamukti yoga, and astanga yoga, are very vigorous. Others, like integral yoga and Kripalu yoga, are slower and more meditative. Some classes are freestyle and eclectic, while Iyengar is formal and precise. The idea behind all these forms, however, is not to transcend or renounce the body but to develop it fully, as a vessel or container for the experience of sacred union. As the *Upanishads*, a classic Vedic text, puts it:

> *The liberation that is attainable by the shedding of the body—is not that liberation worthless? Just as rock salt [is dissolved] in water, so the Absolute* (brahmatva) *extends to the body.*

Yoga adepts often perform prodigious feats of physical prowess, twisting themselves into pretzels or standing on their heads for hours. But these extremes are not the point, nor are the paranormal powers known as *siddhis*—levitation and psychic abilities—that come as a by-product of extended practice. The main idea behind the various *asanas*, or postures, and *pranayama*—breathing practice—is to develop balance and harmony of the body-mind.

Yoga *vinyasas*—sequences of movement done with complete mindfulness—are excellent meditations for anyone too active to stick with a sitting practice, or as an adjunct to sitting. A nice morning meditation is the series of postures known as the Sun Salutation or Salute to the Sun (see page 170). Once you have mastered the asanas,

Try This: Salute to the Sun

Ideally, this *vinyasa*, or devotional practice, is performed in the morning, facing east, toward the rising sun. It gives us an opportunity to honor the natural force that makes life on earth possible, giving us light and warmth and food. The postures themselves stretch and tone all muscles and organs in the body. Use a yoga mat or carpeted floor.

1. Stand up straight and bring your feet together.
2. Bring your hands into prayer position at the center of your chest, with the fingers pointing up.
3. Inhale, lock your thumbs, extend your arms straight out, and raise them over your head, arching your back slightly.
4. Exhale and, with your arms close to your ears, bend forward from the waist, keeping your knees straight (but not locked) and dropping your hands toward the floor.
5. Inhale, place your hands on the floor on either side of your feet, with the finger-tips aligned with your toes.
6. Exhale and extend your left leg behind you, placing your toes on the floor. Raise your chin and look up.
7. Inhaling, extend your right leg in line with the left and hold your arms straight as if you were doing push-ups.
8. Exhale, lower your knees, chest, and chin to the floor, keeping your pelvis raised slightly.
9. Inhale, lower your pelvis to the floor and lift the front part of your body, arching your back slightly and supporting your torso on your outstretched arms. Look up.
10. Exhale, and lift your hips so that your legs and arms form a V. Look back toward your feet.
11. Inhale, and bring your right leg forward, next to your hands, leaving your left leg extended behind you. Look up.

> 12. Exhale and bring your left leg forward next to the right leg.
> 13. Inhale, uncurl to a standing position, and bring your hands to your chest in the prayer position.
> 14. Exhale, separate your legs slightly, and drop your arms to your sides.
> 15. Repeat, performing as one continuous movement.

you can vary the speed at which you perform them. One morning you might feel like a slow, balletlike meditation; the next, an athletic workout.

While you are learning yoga, it can be helpful to attend a class, or practice along with audiotaped or videotaped instructions from an expert. Some people also like to do their asanas to music. (For suggestions, see "Resources.")

T'ai Chi and Chi Kung

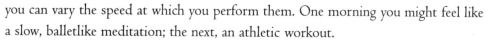

Every morning, town plazas and parks all over China are filled with hundreds of people performing the slow, ritualized movements of the martial art known as t'ai chi ch'uan, usually referred to as t'ai chi (TIE-CHEE). Increasingly, you can find similar activities in Western cities. At San Francisco's Japan Center, for example, the group of practitioners often includes businessmen and -women in suits, elderly Chinese and Japanese in traditional dress, college students in jeans, and camera-wielding tourists from nearby hotels.

Classes in t'ai chi are offered in *dojos* (practice halls) and health clubs. Although it can be challenging to learn t'ai chi properly without a teacher—the "long form" is a sequence of one hundred or more different movements and the short form, twenty-four—it is possible to make a start on your own, with the help of a video or book.

T'ai chi, literally "the way of the fist," grew out of qi gong, or chi kung (pronounced CHEE-GUNG), an ancient Taoist healing system similar to yoga that emphasizes exercise and proper breathing to stimulate the free flow of energy through the body. *Chi* means "energy" and *kung* means "work," or "exercise"; the idea is to balance yin—"feminine," or receptive—energy, with yang—"masculine," or active.

T'ai chi, through a series of movements using the force and counterforce of gravity, brings the body-mind into harmony. Gentle in execution—the movements are slow, deliberate, and flowing—t'ai chi can be done by anyone, regardless of age or physical condition. Nonetheless, it is very powerful as a body toner, as well as a mental and spiritual exercise.

Peter Chin Kean Choy, who has studied with a number of important Taoist masters, created a system called "t'ai chi chi kung," with exercises drawn from both disciplines arranged into programs of different lengths. The five-minute workout starts off with "Spring Chi Kung Exercise," a one-minute sequence that Peter Chin Kean Choy suggests doing on arising or just before leaving home for work. "You will achieve a stronger sense of optimism and joy around you," he explains in *T'ai Chi Chi Kung* (see below).

Try This: Spring Chi Kung Exercise

TIME ALLOTTED: ONE MINUTE

Bring your palms to your heart and stretch them out to the sides slowly and purposefully. The Spring energy is there within you, so that you start the day with a spring of energy inside you. You are like a budding seed opening its seedling case into two halves and stretching to make way for the new to spring up.

—PETER CHIN KEAN CHOY, *T'AI CHI CHI KUNG: FIFTEEN WAYS TO A HAPPIER YOU*

Aikido

Like t'ai chi the Japanese martial art of aikido (EYE-KEE-DO) is based on flowing, circular movements. Its purpose is spiritual development, not foiling an attacker. As its founder, Morihei Ueshiba, described it, aikido is "the way to reconcile the world and make humans one family." In *The Way of Aikido* author and *sensei* (teacher) George Leonard explains what distinguishes aikido from other martial arts. The aikidoist doesn't meet an attack with force or resistance or avoidance, he says,

> *but rather* enters *and* blends. *That is, he or she moves toward the incoming energy and then, at the last instant, slightly off the line of attack, turns so as to look momentarily at the situation* from the attacker's standpoint. *From this position many possibilities exist, including a good chance of reconciliation.*

It is this practice of empathy—of seeing from another person's perspective—that makes aikido such a powerful practice for daily living. If, for example, you receive a verbal attack, instead of striking back you can "blend" by acknowledging your attacker's point of view without giving up your own. "This response," Leonard notes, "is quite disarming, leaving the attacker with no target to focus on." In that moment options open up, including the possibility of reaching an agreement that will satisfy both people's needs.

Unlike t'ai chi or yoga aikido is generally practiced with a partner. However, according to George Leonard, walking can be a good way to practice basic aikido principles, including centering yourself and developing *zanshin*—"continuing awareness."

The following suggestions for doing the aikido walk are based on Leonard's instructions in *The Way of Aikido:*

Stand straight with your feet shoulder-width apart. Breathe deeply, allowing the breath to sink into your pelvis. Imagine a beam of energy coming down through your body, connecting you to the earth.

Close your eyes and rock gently from side to side, making sure that your weight is evenly distributed between your right foot and left, and between the ball and heel of each foot. Move your head gently forward and back and side to side, making sure that your neck and facial muscles are fully relaxed.

Inhale deeply through your nose, raise your shoulders toward your ears, then exhale through your mouth, releasing the tension throughout your body. Open your eyes, maintaining a soft gaze. Rotate your body from side to side at the hips, then stop and shake out your hands, spreading your fingers wide.

Slap each thigh two or three times just below the hipbone. Then reach behind you and tap the small of your back with your fist.

Now, start walking in a comfortable, relaxed stride, breathing naturally and maintaining awareness of the surface under your feet. Gradually shift your awareness to your *hara* (a spot in your abdomen just below your navel); think of this point as your center. Expand your awareness to include your hips and lower back. Lower your center of gravity ever so slightly. "This 'getting down,'" Leonard says, "is an essential el-

Try This: Walking Through Eternity

Set aside a five-to-ten-minute period during your walk. Imagine that the way you walk during that period is the way you will be walking through all of eternity. This will encourage you to choose the way you will be walking through eternity by walking that way now. During the first part of the exercise, bring to mind all the things about your walk that you want to change. You might say to yourself, for example:

"If I'm walking with my head thrust forward now, my head will be thrust forward through all of eternity. I can choose to change that now."

"If I'm walking with an unpleasant expression on my face, I'll have an unpleasant expression on my face for all of eternity. I can choose to change that now."

After going through all the negative factors about your walk that you'd like to change and doing your best to change them, start making positive statements to yourself. For example:

"If my breathing is relaxed and generous now, it will be relaxed and generous through all of eternity!"

—GEORGE LEONARD, *THE WAY OF AIKIDO*

ement for success, not only in Aikido but in all physical activities that involve walking or running."

Once you are comfortable with basic Aikido walking, you can add visualization techniques, Leonard suggests. One exercise, "Walking Through Eternity" (see page 174), helps us see clearly our basic posture toward the world and allows us to choose the attitude we want to carry into the future.

"Aikido is an optimistic martial art, an art based on love and the loving protection of all beings," Leonard emphasizes. "Centered, grounded, graceful, confident walking can be said to create a field of energy that might well gladden the heart of anyone you encounter."

Bowing

Another way to generate positive energy for yourself and others is through an ancient practice followed in many traditions—bowing. Bowing is a way of showing respect, and expressing reverence and gratitude. For Westerners it can be very humbling; bowing when we greet one another is not part of our custom, as it is in many Eastern countries. We tend to forget that bowing is really no different from kneeling in prayer.

Perhaps because it *is* so foreign to many of us, bowing can be an especially powerful spiritual practice. When you enter and leave a Hindu or Buddhist temple, or approach the altar to leave an offering, it is customary to bow. Protocol even calls for bowing to your Zen cushion before you sit down—a sign of appreciation for the seat of your potential enlightenment.

In formal Buddhist circles prostrations—full bows with the head and body touching the ground—are an important part of ritual. When you enter and leave *dokusan*—an audience with a Zen teacher—it is customary to do a series of bows, touching your forehead to the floor. The prostrations are repeated three times—once to the Buddha, once to the Dharma (the teaching), and the third time, to the Sangha—the community of fellow seekers. In *Zen: Dawn in the West* Philip Kapleau Roshi recalls his initial resistance to bowing as a young student. Finally one day his teacher pointed out that Kapleau was not bowing down before the teacher but in fact, honoring his own buddha-nature. Zen teaches that prostration practice is a good way to discover that your own true nature and that of the Buddha are inseparable.

Tibetan Buddhists honor Buddha, Dharma, and Sangha by putting their palms together and touching the forehead, throat, then heart chakra as they make their prostrations. Bowing is taken very seriously in Tibetan Buddhist practice. Lama Surya Das points out in *Awakening to the Sacred* that a new student may be assigned to complete 111,000 prostrations within the first few months.

Clearly, for most people, that practice would be extreme. But if you rebel against the very idea of bowing, think of it as another form of mindfulness training. Surya Das explains:

> [Bowing is] a centering practice that reminds us to divest ourselves of the more worldly personas that we carry around with us as we walk around playing out our roles in the world. When we bow, we lower our guard and surrender to our spiritual nature.

Dhikr and Whirling

Surrendering to our spiritual nature—to the Beloved in our hearts—is the core of Sufi practice. "The Sufi aspires to remember God in every moment, with each and every breath," teacher and author Llewellyn Vaughan-Lee explains in *Sufism: The Transformation of the Heart.* Unlike many other meditation practices Sufi *dhikr* combines body movements with repeating a mantra or the name of God. Devotees dip and sway to the rhythm of the chant. "Through the dhikr," Vaughan-Lee says, "we attune our whole being to the frequency of love." There's an old Sufi saying, he tells us: "First you do the dhikr and then it does you."

The basic practice, as Pir Vilayat describes it in *Awakening*, involves "using our bodies as temples . . . with our heart as the altar." Sitting cross-legged in meditation pose repeat the phrase *La illaha illa 'llah hu*—"There is no God except God"—synchronizing it with the movements of your head. As you exhale, repeat, *"La illaha"* while rotating your head to the left, then down toward your left knee, across to your right knee and up to your right shoulder. Then, as you inhale, repeat, *"Illa 'llah hu"* as you lower your head toward your chest, then raise it straight up so that you are looking toward the ceiling. "The beauty of this practice," states Pir Vilayat, "is that the whole body participates in the mystical experience of the Divine."

Perhaps the best-known Sufi practice is also one of the most beautiful—the trance dance of the dervishes. The Mevlevi order of the Whirling Dervishes was founded by the Sufi mystic and poet Jalaluddin Rumi, in thirteenth-century Turkey. (*Dervish* means "doorway," signifying that the dervish is a realized being who stands in the space where the human and divine meet.) Rumi was a prominent scholar with many followers when his world was turned upside down by the wandering dervish Shams of Tabriz. Rumi's utter devotion to his spiritual master broke open his heart and plunged him "into the fire of divine transformation," as the mystic and poet Andrew Harvey describes it in *The Way of Passion.* Rumi later wrote, "My whole life is condensed in these . . . words: I was raw, now I am cooked and burnt."

Try This: Whirling

Whirling is a sacred ritual that is an extremely powerful way to merge with the divine. Here are the basic steps.

1. Stand with your weight on your left foot. Begin whirling by rotating counterclockwise on the ball of your left foot. (Traditionally, a nail in the floor between the dervish's big toe and second toe served as a pivot point.) Use your right foot to push off and to maintain your balance when necessary.
2. Unfocus your eyes and keep a soft gaze as you turn. Be sure not to "spot" that is, do not focus on any single point.
3. Once your turning is established, slowly raise your arms and hold them out straight at shoulder height. The palm of the right hand should be turned upward, to receive spirit. The palm of the left hand should be turned down, to guide spirit to earth. If you become too dizzy, focus on the knuckle of your left index finger.
4. When you are ready to stop, pick a spot on the wall, then stand still and stare at the spot until the room stops spinning and your body comes to rest.

For months Rumi lived in an ecstatic state, inseparable from his spiritual friend. Such was their love, it is said, that it was never clear who was the lover and who the beloved. Then, suddenly, Shams disappeared. Rumi was devastated. In one version of the story Rumi, in his grief, began whirling, and as he whirled, poetry poured out of him. Shams returned, only to disappear again—murdered, it is thought, by Rumi's jealous students with the help of Rumi's son. But the "fire of longing" for the Beloved—God—raged on in Rumi, and the Mevlevi order of Whirling Dervishes was born. (*Mevlevi* comes from the Turkish word meaning "wherever you turn, you see God.").

Whirling invites you to lose yourself in the dance and turn to the divine. In *The Call of the Dervish* Pir Vilayat likens it to "the whirling of the planets" and the dance of Shiva. "It's ecstasy, of course; it's a kind of wine," he says. Whirling is the cosmic dance, a moving metaphor for the rotation of the planets around the sun. "The dhikr dance opens us up to planetary emotion, instead of the emotion of the individual," Pir Vilayat explains. "It's part of what's called group consciousness."

Sacred Dance

Other traditions also have their own forms of ritual and ecstatic dance—all of which have a powerful effect in creating sacred union. Think of a Wiccan circle "raising the cone of power" or a tribal shamanic healing rite.

One of the most uplifting and enjoyable ways to "pray with your body" is to follow the path of movement as sacred practice laid out by the teacher, performer, and recording artist Gabrielle Roth. "I want to focus on ways we can retrieve our souls through our bodies," she writes in her most recent book, *Sweat Your Prayers*. "Not in spite of our bodies or instead of our bodies, but through the very flesh that defines our presence on this plane of reality." Roth defines the essence of the "dancing path":

My bible is the body because the body can't lie. My master is rhythm. . . . When you let your body dance, you immediately strip away the lies and the dogma until all you're left with is the spirit of life itself.

Roth calls her physical/spiritual workout the Wave, based on the Five Rhythms (see page 180). "Doing the rhythms," she explains, "is about waking up to your most essential nature, stretching your intuition and imagination as surely as your body." Each of the rhythms is distinct, its essence discernible from its name: flowing, staccato, chaos, lyrical, stillness. There is no set routine you must follow; Roth encourages you to listen to your body and give it the rhythm and pace it requires.

"The Wave . . . is a flexible practice, meant to reflect the level of your energy rather than force you to conform to it as a rigid discipline," she explains. "Although there are five rhythms, today you may only do one and tomorrow you may do three." Like any spiritual practice it requires a commitment "to show up." But to Roth it is unimportant whether you work out for five minutes or an hour.

One woman who first learned the Five Rhythms in Gabrielle Roth's workshop at a Body & Soul Conference (see "Resources") recalls the life-changing effect that even one session can have. "I cried, I laughed, I felt joy, and in the end, a kind of free-floating gratitude just for being alive. I've done a lot of movement work, but I'd never before seen it so clearly as a spiritual exercise."

People who find going to the gym a bore and have difficulty sticking with an exercise program often resonate with the Five Rhythms because its philosophy is nonjudgmental and life affirming. A buff body isn't required, but it is often a by-product of ongoing practice. Two women in one of Roth's recent workshops each reported losing over a hundred pounds since starting to do the rhythms four or five mornings a week a year earlier. Such testimonials are not unusual, Roth says. By itself, doing the rhythms does not guarantee dramatic weight loss, but trance dancing can lift depression and raise self-esteem, providing the boost someone needs to stick to a diet and self-care program.

Ultimately, Roth's intention isn't to promote weight loss but spiritual development. The Wave is a spiritual practice, and the rhythms are catalysts for deep changes in the psyche. Commenting on Roth's work, theologian Matthew Fox said, "Dance deserves to be called 'the yoga of the West.' "

Try This: Doing the Five Rhythms

Over the years I discovered the five sacred rhythms that are the essence of the body in motion, the body alive: Flowing, Staccato, Chaos, Lyrical, Stillness.

1. *Flowing:* Picture yourself in your room alone, about to pray. Imagine a gentle drumbeat and feel your breath rising and sinking with it, expanding and contracting. A rolling drumbeat captures your feet. You go with this flowing rhythm, enhance it, exaggerate it: inhaling, rising, expanding, opening; then exhaling, sinking, contracting, closing. There are no sharp edges to your movement, only curves, endless circles of motion, each gesture evolving into the next. Your body has become a sea of waves, flowing in all directions.

2. *Staccato:* The drums intensify. The pulsing of the bass grabs your belly and you begin to move in sharp, staccato, defined ways. Your arms and legs become percussive instruments. Your body's jerking, jabbing, jamming, falling into patterns and repeating them over and over till they die and a new pattern is born.

3. *Chaos:* Now the beat builds, the pace quickens. You dance over the edge into chaos. You're swept up in some primal rite, falling deeper and deeper into yourself, an intuitive stream of essential movements. Your body is gyrating, limp as a rag doll, spine undulating, head loose, hands flying. You're electric, turned on, plugged into something huge. You are vibrantly alive.

4. *Lyrical:* The drums lighten up, and your body shifts into the trancelike state of the lyrical rhythm—grounded but soaring. There is a lightness of being in your feet, a sense of being airborne. Your body sweeps in graceful loops like a bird in the wind, bouncing, darting, dipping, diving.

5. *Stillness:* Finally, stillness enters your dance, calling you into spaces between the beats. Your attention is drawn to your inner dance, where everything is alive, awake, aware. You have disappeared into the dance, and the dance has disappeared in you. Picture yourself sitting doing nothing, just being.

—ADAPTED FROM *MAPS TO ECSTASY* BY GABRIELLE ROTH

[For suggestions on music to accompany your practice, see "Resources."]

Celebrating the Techno Cosmic Mass

If anyone understands the role of rhythm and movement in spiritual practice, it's Matthew Fox, a postmodern priest who devised the Techno Cosmic Mass—a multisensory, multicultural, multimedia event with slide shows, synthesizers, shamanic rituals, and rock music that owes as much to the all-night music fests known as "raves" as it does to Western liturgical tradition. With its mix of ecstatic music and dance, visual imagery, and Eastern, Western, and indigenous spiritual elements, the experience, its organizers say, "brings the body back into worship."

That's an understatement. Imagine a hotel ballroom or church basement with high-tech sound equipment blasting out percussion and digitally composed dance music, multiple screens flashing computer-generated pictures, a full-blown light show, and in the center of it all, an altar-in-the-round festooned with flowers, fruits, religious icons, and natural objects—all presided over by priests dressed like rock musicians in multicolored shirts and robes, celebrating an ecumenical mass. Meanwhile, all around them are congregants in various states of bliss, many of them barefoot and in jeans or workout clothes, dancing themselves into a frenzy.

Contrary to appearances this is no out-of-control orgy but a carefully orchestrated, futuristic version of the ritual mass. Like its traditional counterpart the Techno Cosmic Mass has as its purpose bringing together the community to, as Fox's Web site puts it, "experience a common story, bring praise and thanksgiving to the Creator, and through communion, offer spiritual sustenance for works of compassion and justice to the world."

A controversial Catholic-turned-Episcopalian who is founder of the University of Creation Spirituality in Oakland, California, Matthew Fox is well known for his efforts to reintegrate spirit and body—the body politic and body of the earth, as well as the human body. The Techno Cosmic Mass—inspired by the Planetary Mass (also called Rave Mass) first organized in England—takes its name, according to Fox, from efforts to explore how technology can "contribute to bringing about a sense of the sacred." Each of the four parts of the mass represents one of the spiritual paths embodied in Creation Spirituality: *via positiva*, the path of awe, wonder, and joy; *via negativa*, the path of loss and letting go; *via creativa*, the path of renewal and creative expression; and *via transformativa*, the path of compassionate action and celebration. Like the spiritual circus of the Medieval cathedral this mass is a giant tent under which all seekers are welcome to come and worship. For movers and shakers, dancers and dreamers, here is the ultimate proof of the embodied soul, of spirit in action. To paraphrase Thich Nhat Hanh: Every step is a prayer.

RESOURCES

BOOKS

Artress, Dr. Lauren. *Walking a Sacred Path.* New York: Riverhead, 1995.

Chin Kean Choy, Peter. *T'ai Chi Chi Kung.* New York: Overlook Press, 1999.

Cousineau, Phil. *The Art of Pilgrimage.* Berkeley: Conari, 1998.

Das, Lama Surya. *Awakening to the Sacred.* New York: Broadway, 1999.

Fadiman, James, and Robert Frager. *Essential Sufism.* San Francisco: Harper San Francisco, 1997.

Feuerstein, Georg. *The Yoga Tradition.* Prescott, Ariz.: Hohm Press, 1998.

Fox, Matthew. *Sins of the Spirit, Blessings of the Flesh.* New York: Harmony, 1999.

Garripoli, Garri, and friends. *Qigong: Essence of the Healing Dance.* Deerfield Beach, Fl.: Health Communications, 1999.

Housden, Roger. *Sacred Journeys in a Modern World.* New York: Simon & Schuster, 1998.

Jaskolski, Helmut. *The Labyrinth.* Boston: Shambhala, 1997.

Kapleau, Philip, Roshi. *Zen: Dawn in the West.* New York: Doubleday, 1979.

Kapleau, Philip, ed. *The Three Pillars of Zen.* Boston: Beacon, 1965.

Khan, Pir Vilayat Inayat. *Awakening: A Sufi Experience.* New York: Jeremy P. Tarcher, 1999.

———. *The Call of the Dervish.* Indianapolis: Omega Publications, 1981.

Leonard, George. *The Way of Aikido.* New York: Dutton, 1999.

Mundy, Linus. *The Complete Guide to Prayer-Walking.* New York: Crossroad, 1996.

Nhat Hahn, Thich. *The Miracle of Mindfulness.* Boston: Beacon, 1976.

————. *Present Moment, Wonderful Moment.* Berkeley: Parallax Press, 1990.

Rolheiser, Ronald. *The Holy Longing.* New York: Doubleday, 1999.

Roth, Gabrielle. *Maps to Ecstasy.* Novato, Cal.: New World Library, 1998.

————. *Sweat Your Prayers.* New York: Jeremy P. Tarcher/Putnam, 1997.

The Upanishads. New York: New American Library, 1990.

Vaughan-Lee, Llewellyn. *Sufism: The Transformation of the Heart.* Inverness, Cal.: The Golden Sufi Center, 1995.

Wakefield, Dan. *How Do We Know When It's God?* New York: Little, Brown, 1999.

Yount, David. *Breaking Through God's Silence.* New York: Touchstone, 1996.

PERIODICALS

A Moving Journal
168 Fourth Street
Providence, RI 02906
(401) 274–2765

Yoga Journal
2054 University Avenue, Suite 302
Berkeley, CA 94704
(510) 841–9200

AUDIO/VIDEO

African Healing Dance. Wyoma and the Damballa dance troupe. Instructional tape (Sounds True). VHS

Chakra Yoga. Gurutej Kaur. Dynamic postures and sacred chants to release energy blocks (Sounds True). VHS.

Labyrinths: Their Mystery and Magic. How-to workshops, lectures, and interviews on this ancient transformational tool, taped at the 1996 National Labyrinth Conference at Omega Institute (Penny Price Media). VHS

Mevlana: Music of the Whirling Dervishes. Sacred music of the mystical order (Hemisphere).

Mindful Movements. Gentle exercises led by Vietnamese Zen master Thich Nhat Hanh and monks and nuns of Plum Village (Sounds True). VHS

Mudra, Gestures of Power. Sabrina Mesko. Instructions on using yogic "seals" (Sounds True). VHS

The Practice of Qigong. Ken Cohen. Intensive course on this healing art, including twenty-five meditation exercises (Sounds True).

Qigong. Ken Cohen. Instructions on harnessing the power of *qi,* universal energy (Sounds True). VHS

Trance 1. Sufi dervish rite, Tibetan overtone chanting, and *dhrupad,* Indian classical music (Ellipsis Art).

Trance 2. Sufi dhikr, Moroccan healing rites, and Balinese temple music (Ellipsis Art).

The Wave. Gabrielle Roth and the Mirrors. Ecstatic dance for body and soul, with Tibetan chants and percussion (Raven).

WEB SITES

www.creationspirituality.com

Friends of Creation Spirituality Web site, offering the Original Blessing network newsletter and information on educational programs, the Techno Cosmic Mass, and theologian Matthew Fox, founder and president of the University of Creation Spirituality in Oakland, Cal.

www.ravenrecording.com

Information on workshop and training schedules, and recordings by performer/ teacher/author Gabrielle Roth, creator of the Roth 5 Rhythms.

Three

❖

Coming
Home

10.

Staying on the Path

*True fearlessness is not the reduction of fear,
but going beyond fear.*

—CHÖGYAM TRUNGPA

Just as peace and joy are a part of the contemplative life,
so are doubt, anger, and frustration. Nothing brings us
closer to our humanity than meditation and prayer. As
you spend time on your spiritual journey, you will at
some point encounter what Insight meditation teacher
Sylvia Boorstein calls "the pain that comes from being a
human being living in a human body." This is the darkness Job describes when he calls out to God, "I cry to
you, and you give me no answer; I stand before you, but
you take no notice."

Feelings like these may emerge without warning, just
when your practice—and your life—seem to be moving along nicely. One morning,
the songbirds that once seemed to celebrate God's creation will suddenly sound
raucous and grating. Or the thoughts that stream through your mind as you sit in

meditation will astonish you with their vehemence. The very existence of dark clouds in your clear consciousness may feel like a betrayal of your spiritual commitment.

Do not quit now, even if the temptation is great. Frustration, discouragement, and doubts—even grave ones—are part of the journey.

Much as we'd like to think the way should be smooth, there is no such thing as instant enlightenment. Rabbi David A. Cooper warns against this delusion—what he calls "hula hoop spirituality." Others have dubbed this desire for the quick-and-easy route, "spirituality lite."

The truth is, any change is hard, and spiritual enfoldment is no exception. At the beginning of a Zen *sesshin*—an intense, seven-day silent retreat—it is not uncommon to hear the retreat leader repeat the Buddha's words as encouragement: "Hard it is to be born; harder still, to be born human. Do your best!"

Luckily we don't realize at the beginning of our journey the challenges we are likely to encounter along the way. By the time the going gets tough, we have developed enough spiritual "muscle" to keep practicing despite our resistance. Zen master Eido Shimano Roshi predicts, "If you sit for seven years, you'll sit for a lifetime." For many of us in our instant-coffee society, seven years *seems* like a lifetime. "Do your best!" is a good reminder whenever your will momentarily flags.

It is not easy to be with the self in silence, as that is where our most painful thoughts and feelings emerge. In fact, these uncomfortable thoughts are often the reason we create such busy lives: we think we can outrun inner discomfort. Our culture supports us in this denial. "Just keep busy, and you'll feel better," we tell the person who's angry or grieving or afraid. We feed the same advice to ourselves.

When our lives are full of activity, we can trick ourselves into believing that our difficulties are the result of whatever we're doing or whomever we're doing it with. Once we slow down and create time for stillness, we discover that it is not what happens but our reaction to it that causes our inner pain.

Most of us assume that following a spiritual path will offer relief from suffering. But the truth is: When we open the door to our own spirit, we open it to all of life— pleasures, pains, joys, and sorrows.

Space for Spirit

Spiritual unfolding creates inner space. As Pema Chödrön, the American Buddhist nun who directs Gampo Abbey in Nova Scotia, explains in *Everyday Mind: 366 Reflections on the Buddhist Path,*

> *that sounds good, but actually it can be unnerving, because when there's a lot of space you can see very clearly: you've removed your veils, your shields, your armor, your dark glasses, your earplugs, your layers of mittens, your heavy boots. Finally you're standing, touching the earth, feeling the sun on your body, feeling its brightness, hearing all the noises without anything to dull the sound. . . . Since meditation has this quality of bringing you very close to yourself and your experience, you tend to come up against your edge faster. It's not an edge that wasn't there before, but because things are so simplified and clear, you see it, and you see it vividly.*

This is the point at which many of us stop praying, or meditating, or taking time to be still. Though undoubtedly there is something welcoming in this "open space" that Pema Chödrön speaks of, there may also be a lot we don't want to see. There may even be nothing at all—a frightening prospect in itself. One woman recalls the panic she felt midway through a seven-day Zen retreat. As her mind calmed and she began to lose the obsessive thoughts she habitually clung to, she began to fear that underneath all the chatter in her mind, she was totally empty. And to her, emptiness meant death.

What we don't know is what frightens us. "The essential power of doubt is the unknown; it cannot exist in the face of truth," writes Rabbi David A. Cooper in *A Heart of Stillness.* "Thus, every time we step into the unknown, we encounter doubt in its fullest intensity."

It is in such times of uncertainty that it is most important to trust. If we can't yet trust ourselves, we can trust the process of unfolding to help us stay on the path. The theologian Matthew Fox notes that the word Jesus used most often for *faith* means "trust" in the original Greek *(pisteuein)*. As the medieval German mystic Hildegarde of Bingen expressed it, "Trust shows the way." We develop trust, quips the writer

Stephen Levine, when we see that doubt is "just another of the top forty hits of the mind game."

Dealing with it is a matter of turning the dial.

Facing Doubt

If you seesaw between faith ("This is great, I'm on the right path") and doubt ("This is scary, count me out"), you're joining a long line of seekers. When the ancient Hebrews made their exodus to Egypt, the first enemy they encountered was the kingdom of Amalek, which God commanded them to destroy. Amalek, according to Kabbalist scholars, is a synonym for *suffek*, which means "doubt." Doubt is the first adversary of the spiritual life.

The First Noble Truth taught by the Buddha is that life is *dukkha*. Often translated as "suffering," *dukkha* literally means "frustrating" or "hollow." "Buddha dharma does not teach that everything is suffering," Lama Surya Das writes in *Awakening the Buddha Within*. Instead, it teaches that by its very nature, life is "difficult, flawed, imperfect," he explains. "That we all experience ups and downs no matter who we are."

Suffering, the Sri Lankan Buddhist monk Henepola Gunaratana tells us in *Mindfulness in Plain English*, is a result of "the mental treadmill." It is important to remember, he says, that the treadmill is not a product of our spiritual practice but something that is with us every day, all the time. Therefore, the feelings of doubt that arise when you practice are not because of the practice, but because it is only in silence that you become aware of them.

This is what is meant by the phrase *Wherever you go, there you are.* Prayer and meditation do not eliminate feelings of discomfort; rather, through practice we learn how to accept them as part of life. But the process of acceptance takes time, which is why it can be daunting. In *Nothing Special: Living Zen*, Charlotte Joko Beck likens the difficulty to the life cycle of a butterfly:

> *We may imagine, for example, that because butterflies are pretty, their life in the cocoon before they emerge is also pretty. We don't realize all that the worm must go through in order to become a*

butterfly. Similarly, when we begin to practice, we don't realize the long and difficult transformation required of us. We have to see through our pursuit of outward things, the false gods of pleasure and security. We have to stop gobbling this and pursuing that in our shortsighted way, and simply relax into the coccoon, into the darkness of the pain that is our life. Such practice requires years of our lives. Unlike the butterfly we don't emerge once and for all.

Riding Out Difficulties

What should you do in the face of difficulty? The answer is simple, though it may not be easy: Sit with it. Breathe into your discomfort, your doubt, your confusion. Find within yourself the way to let it go.

This part of the journey requires patience—above all, with yourself. In *Everyday Mind: 366 Reflections on the Buddhist Path*, Pema Chödrön compares the experience of confronting discomfort in the midst of spiritual practice to what happens to a river when it suddenly hits a dam:

> *The river flows rapidly down the mountain, and then all of a sudden it gets blocked with big boulders and a lot of trees. The water can't go any farther, even though it has tremendous force and forward energy. It just gets blocked there. That's what happens with us, too; we get blocked like that. Letting go at the end of the out-breath, letting the thoughts go, is like moving one of those boulders away so that the water can keep flowing, so that our energy and our life force can keep evolving and going forward.*

Sometimes the problem is that we're not even sure where it hurts. When students of Insight meditation teacher Sharon Salzberg complain of not being able to meditate, Salzberg explores to find the exact problem. "The difference between what's happening and one's interpretation of it can be vast," she points out.

Perhaps you keep falling asleep when you meditate, so you decide you must be lazy or resistant and, therefore, can't continue. But sometimes, Salzberg says, sleepiness actually denotes *too much* concentration, rather than too little. One of the most effective ways to deal with doubt, she suggests in *A Heart as Wide as the World*, "is to actually use it as the object of mindfulness—to recognize the confusion, the indecision, the questioning, not as authentic inquiry but simply for what they are: doubt. Seeing that, we can remember again our real goal of insight."

Spiritual practice gives us an opportunity to explore the exact nature of our experience moment to moment—to see what's really going on behind our quick fixes and busyness and assumptions about life.

Pain

But what about another hindrance to practice—namely, pain? Emotional pain is one thing, but what about physical discomfort? Even for experienced meditators, sitting still on a little cushion can be uncomfortable after a while. And in the beginning it can be downright excruciating, especially if you are not particularly limber.

Try not to be too quick to give up, even if you experience pain. Believe it or not, pain can be one of your greatest teachers. If you can sit with it for even a few minutes—relax into it, rather than resist it; look at it straight on, rather than letting your mind wander to avoid it—you will find to your astonishment that the nature of the pain changes. It comes and goes. It changes location and intensity. It passes.

Meditation teachers generally recommend that you try not to wiggle about or move during your meditation period. (In communal practice most sessions last between thirty-five minutes and an hour.) This discipline gives you a chance to experience what we're talking about. And if you do move, you'll often find that the discomfort simply follows you. Then, you may set up a vicious circle: Judging yourself lazy or inadequate as a meditator because you moved, you then feel the emotional pain of inadequacy.

A more productive response to life's difficulties—physical or mental—is to "penetrate to their very depth," as Sharon Salzberg puts it in *A Heart as Wide as the World:*

> *Opening to painful experiences does not mean a passive acceptance of pain. Rather, we learn to go to the heart of each moment's experience, even if it is painful, because there—unclouded by conditioning—we discover our lives. The effort to push away what is unpleasant, the tendency to*

project pain into the future and then feel overcome by it, the interpretations we add to it—all keep us from having a personal, direct, and intimate acquaintance with what we're actually experiencing. So, when we observe something like pain directly, we come to see its exact nature: like everything else, pain is a changing phenomenon with no inherent substance.

Pain, doubt, anger, fear, laziness, restlessness—all these internal states can tempt us to abandon spiritual life. Once we begin to see that these hindrances are a normal part of the journey, however, we can begin to trust ourselves to stay with the unfolding process.

Insight meditation teacher and psychologist Jack Kornfield suggests looking carefully at the "story" you tell yourself whenever you encounter discomfort or a bad mood. That story is what's perpetuating the painful feelings. Probably you're saying something along the lines of "I'm a bad person," or "I'll always feel this way." Recognizing the pattern is the beginning of changing it, Kornfield notes in *A Path with Heart.* "The task in meditation is to drop below the level of the repeated recorded message, to sense and feel the energy that brings it up. When we can do this, and truly come to terms with the feeling, the thought will no longer need to arise, and the pattern will naturally fade away."

Expand the field of awareness is the method Kornfield suggests. (This is like Pema Chödrön's suggestion to create a lot of inner space.) "Discover what is asking for acceptance." In other words, what pattern has been locked in by your fear, or avoidance, or judgment? To unlock it you might try one of the heart-centering practices in Chapter 6. "We must inquire," Kornfield proposes, "what aspect of [a] repeated pattern is asking for acceptance and compassion, and ask ourself, 'Can I touch with love whatever I have closed my heart to?' "

It is a spiritual and psychological truth that the devil we know is easier to face than the one we don't. Jack Kornfield has devised a "Meditation on Making the Demons Part of the Path" (see page 194) that allows us to work with whichever of the inner devils—fear, boredom, doubt, restlessness, or lust—is challenging us.

As you continue your practice, there is another sort of devil you might encounter—what the late Tibetan Buddhist teacher Chögyam Trungpa called "spiritual materialism." You've gained a degree of mastery and insight, but now your ego clings to the idea of the progress you've made. "Look how spiritual I am," it screams. As you accumulate more and more spiritual knowledge and experience, you begin to believe *that* is the goal, rather than true liberation and deep awareness. At this point, it's tempting to abandon your practice, thinking you've already got the answer.

Whichever of these devils tempts us to step off the path, we must simply ignore it and plunge ahead. As one ancient master put it, with great awareness comes great doubt. Contemplative living means learning to contain both—to continue our practice in spite of reservations or resistance. The "direct path" to transformation, as Andrew Harvey emphasizes in *Son of Man*, requires that each of us become responsible for his or her own spiritual evolution.

RESOURCES

BOOKS

Beck, Charlotte Joko. *Nothing Special: Living Zen.* San Francisco: Harper San Francisco, 1993.

Boorstein, Sylvia. *Don't Just Do Something, Sit There.* San Francisco: Harper San Francisco, 1996.

Chödrön, Pema. *Start Where You Are.* Boston: Shambhala, 1994.

————. *When Things Fall Apart.* Boston: Shambhala, 1997.

————. *The Wisdom of No Escape.* Boston: Shambhala, 1991.

Cooper, David A. *Entering the Sacred Mountain: Exploring the Mystical Practices of Judaism, Buddhism, and Sufism.* New York: Bell Tower, 1994.

————. *A Heart of Stillness.* Woodstock, Vt.: SkyLight Paths, 1999.

————. *Silence, Simplicity, and Solitude.* Woodstock, Vt.: SkyLight Paths, 1999.

Das, Lama Surya. *Awakening the Buddha Within.* New York: Broadway, 1998.

Harvey, Andrew. *Son of Man.* New York: Tarcher/Putnam, 1998.

Kornfield, Jack. *A Path with Heart.* New York: Bantam, 1993.

Levine, Stephen. *Healing into Life and Death.* New York: Anchor, 1987.

Salzberg, Sharon. *A Heart as Wide as the World.* Boston: Shambhala, 1999.

————. *Lovingkindness.* Boston: Shambhala, 1997.

PERIODICALS

Body and Soul: The Annual Guide to Holistic Living
Published by *New Age* magazine
42 Pleasant Street
Watertown, MA 02472
(617) 926–0200

Common Boundary
7005 Florida Street
Chevy Chase, MD 20815
(301) 652–9495

11.
Creating
Community

All we need to do to receive
direct help is to ask.
—SOGYAL RINPOCHE

The spiritual path may at times be difficult, but there are ways to gather strength for continuing the journey. One is to find a group of like-minded people, a *sangha*—which means "virtuous community" in Sanskrit. Another is to follow the age-old practice of spiritual renewal by going on retreat for a few days, or weeks, or months.

"It is difficult, if not impossible, to practice the way of understanding and love without a *sangha*, a community of friends who practice in the same way," the Vietnamese Zen monk Thich Nhat Hanh writes in *A Joyful Path: Community Transformation and Peace. Sangha* can be created in a prayer circle, a meditation group, a twelve-step meeting, or in any gathering where there is a sense of support and shared commitment that

Try This: Finding a Sangha

"I get by with a little help from my friends," the Beatles sang. And so it is on the spiritual journey. Though ultimately each of us is responsible for his or her own awakening, there is no question that a community of like-minded people can help us sustain our practice even in times of resistance and doubt. Others who are following the same path offer companionship, inspiration, and support. Although the great spiritual leaders—think of Jesus and the Buddha—spent time alone on retreat, they also relied on a *sangha,* or group of spiritual friends and confidants.

In traditional religious circles, the *sangha* is the congregation—the members of a church or synagogue or mosque. But perhaps you're interested in a meditation practice rather than a conventional religious affiliation. How can you find an appropriate group?

+ **Seek referrals**: Ask friends who already have a meditation practice where and with whom they sit.

+ **Check local alternative publications**: Many communities have a newspaper or magazine that lists spiritual groups and activities in the area. You can also consult magazines that cover spiritual topics, such as *Tricycle: The Buddhist Review, Yoga Journal, New Age, Shambhala Sun,* and *Common Boundary.*

+ **Check bulletin boards**: Your local health food store or natural foods restaurant is likely to post notices of meditation groups and retreat centers.

+ **Consult the Resources sections** at the end of this chapter and Chapters 4 and 5 for addresses of spiritual centers and books listing monasteries, abbeys, and retreats.

+ **Go online**: Search the Internet for information on the tradition in which you are interested (e.g., Zen Buddhism, Vipassana, Kabbalah, *Siddha* yoga). A number of web sites list centers geographically.

+ **Start your own**: If you can't find a group in your area, consider starting one. Post a notice, run an ad, tell friends to spread the word. All you need is one other "spiritual friend" and the intention to begin a *sangha.*

Spiritual groups vary widely, of course, in focus and form. Most are organized around a particular teacher or teaching or tradition. They may meet regularly, at a center or set place, or more informally, at the homes of members.

Once you have narrowed your search, you will want to be sure that the group you have selected is ethical in its dealings with its members and the wider community. It is always advisable to visit a group several times before you make any commitment to it. Ask yourself the following questions:

♦ Are members free to come and go from this group?

♦ Do group members show respect and consideration for one another?

♦ Are an individual's rights and opinions respected? Is dissent allowed?

♦ If there is a teacher, is the teacher honorable in his/her dealings with group members? (See **Chapter 2, "Getting Ready"** for suggestions on what to look for and what to avoid in a spiritual teacher.)

Finally, keep in mind that if the group doesn't feel right to you for any reason, leave. Only you can decide which is the right path to lead you to inner freedom.

sustains the members on the spiritual journey. This is what Jesus meant when he said, "Where two or more are gathered in my name, there shall I be also." Although more and more people these days are turning to prayer and meditation—and openly discussing their practices with friends—in the beginning we may be reluctant to reveal our experiences to people who may not be supportive. As Lama Surya Das points out in *Awakening to the Sacred*, "Seekers need spiritual friends. Even the awakened Buddha reached out to others who shared his priorities and interests."

And a *sangha* provides not only spiritual friends but also mentors, notes Surya Das. "It's encouraging and inspiring to spend time with men and women who are farther along on the spiritual path. We learn by their example and are buoyed up and carried along by their living presence in our lives."

Rabbi Zalman Shachter-Shalom calls the experience of *sangha* "socialized meditation" and says that the communal experience is what deepens practice. "When people pray, meditate, and share their inner process together, it creates a shift. So instead of thinking of 'I, I' you're thinking of 'us, we.' "

The people in a *sangha* are generally united by their common devotion or practice or spiritual commitment. But they are also individuals—often from strikingly differ- ent backgrounds—and this diversity will color the life and direction of the group. "Members can create new forms of prayer, ritual, and togetherness from their disparate backgrounds and beliefs," explains Holly Bridges, author of *A Circle of Prayer: Coming Together to Find Spirit, Caring, and Community.* "A caring group is a treasure," she observes, "but such groups do not arise miraculously. Rather, they take conscious effort." For suggestions on locating a spiritual community, see "Finding a *Sangha*," page 197.

Retreat Centers

Another place to allow the experience of community to support and deepen your spir- itual experience is at a retreat center or monastery. A spiritual retreat, as Rabbi David A. Cooper notes in *Silence, Simplicity, and Solitude,* can "traverse the internal barriers of our fixed ideas and open the gates of wisdom."

One of the most eloquent explorers of the contemporary monastic experience was the Trappist monk Thomas Merton, who wrote widely on contemplative life before he died suddenly in 1968. Merton called monastic life "a prolonged prayer in which the monk remains united with God through all his occupations." The writer Kathleen Norris, who has spent much time in Benedictine cloisters, in her first experience at a convent retreat found herself "immersed in the kind of silence that sinks to your bones," she writes in *Dakota: A Spiritual Geography.* "I felt as if I was breathing deeply for the first time in years."

Often people think, *Oh, I couldn't go to a monastery or convent or retreat center. They're only for the spiritually committed or the devout.* In some cases it's just the opposite. As a forty-year- old former mathematics professor living in a Zen monastery once explained, "Look, if I was more certain of my commitment, I wouldn't be here. I came here because I needed an environment that would support my practice and eliminate some of the distractions."

As anyone who's lived in a spiritual community knows, you do not escape yourself—or the ups and downs of ordinary human interaction—just because you spend much or all of your time in silence. But a visit to a place that is dedicated to contemplative living generally offers a glimpse of the level of serenity you can achieve with continued practice. As Father Thomas Keating, who lives at St. Benedict's Monastery in Snowmass, Colorado, observes, "More people than ever seem to be hungry for the peace we are blessed with every day."

Most contemplative communities follow a simple schedule of prayer or meditation interspersed with meals, work periods, study or teaching, and time for rest and reflection. The rituals and even the space itself can deepen your spiritual experience. Along with the prescribed daily schedule, they allow you to focus within, rather than on the demands and distractions that occupy most of ordinary life.

"The bells, drums, and sounding boards of a Buddhist community articulate and relate space and events," observes Richard Baker Roshi, a founder of the Tassajara Zen Mountain Center in California, an affiliate of the San Francisco Zen Center. Bells signal the beginning and end of meditation periods; gongs call you to meals. The only sounds that break the silence, they punctuate the activities of the day. Ideally, the physical design of the retreat center also supports your practice. "The space of physical passages should be designed according to what will be done there—people walking slowly and quietly, for example," Baker Roshi explains. "Stone walkways can bring you the long way around a building so that you can change your pace and enter the building with familiarity."

One woman who lived in a Zen monastery in upstate New York that was modeled on a National Treasure *zendo* in Japan, recalls that the beauty of the architecture and the sense of order it conveyed helped her stay with the practice. "Even when my frustration made me question the difficulty of the meditation and the rigor of monastic life, I never lost the feeling of awe and grace when I entered the *zendo* or walked across the porch to meals. Twenty years later I can still smell the temple incense and hear the reverberation of the big gong sounding for evening service."

The Spirit of Intimacy

There is a particular kind of intimacy that arises from being on retreat together that is unlike any other. In *Silence, Simplicity, and Solitude,* David Cooper describes the atmosphere toward the end of a hundred-day silent *Vipassana* (Insight meditation) retreat. "Fellow retreatants do not have to speak with one another to make an acquaintance; something happens on a more essential level than verbal communication. We can sense when things are in balance," he explains. "We know that our struggles are common experiences."

You do not have to take monastic vows or participate in a formal Zen or *Vipassana* training period to share the intimacy Cooper describes or experience the power and immediacy of living in a community focused on spiritual practice. There is a wide variety of centers and monasteries and convents that welcome visitors for guided programs or individual retreats. (See page 205 for suggestions.) Most centers, even those with a religious affiliation, are open to people of any faith. Monasteries and abbeys are usually functioning religious communities that have set aside some rooms for visitors. You may be invited to participate in services and at least some aspects of communal life. Other retreat centers may offer courses or programs with a spiritual focus. The Insight Meditation Society in Barre, Massachusetts, for example, provides meditation instruction and retreats of varying lengths, with a prescribed schedule that the entire group follows. Down the street, at the Barre Center for Buddhist Studies, there are talks and courses on the dharma—teachings of the Buddha—in a less-structured setting.

If you prefer to create a more personal retreat on your own timetable, a community such as Marie Joseph Spiritual Center in Biddeford, Maine, might be more appropriate. The center provides a simple room and invites guests to prayer sessions and meals, but otherwise you are on your own.

With the increasing popularity of spiritual practice and retreat, many centers are booked far in advance, so it is wise to plan ahead. Each community has its own rules and customs, so be sure to check and see if the guidelines are ones you are willing to follow (see "Checklist for Retreats," page 202). Part of the learning experience of living in community is watching how you deal with people and customs not necessarily

Inspiration: Checklist for Retreats

Going on retreat is a chance to "get away from it all," an opportunity for rest and renewal. But if your retreat takes you to a spiritual community, there are likely to be suggestions or rules you will be expected to follow, out of consideration for other retreatants and for the smooth functioning of the community as a whole.

Before you visit a spiritual community, be sure to ask for guidelines about behavior appropriate to that particular center. If you do not think you can follow the rules, pick another place.

+ *Silence:* Many monasteries, convents, and retreat centers maintain silence for all or part of the day. You may be expected to keep silence for days or even weeks, depending on the length of your retreat. Practice silence at home for a day if you've never tried it (see "Noble Silence," Chapter 3, page 46).

+ *Appropriate dress:* Scanty clothing and brief bathing suits are inappropriate for spiritual communities. Find out what other clothing guidelines you should observe. Some retreat centers require robes for meditation. Will a robe be available for you to borrow, if you do not have your own?

+ *What to take:* Warm clothing for cool evenings, hiking or walking shoes, rain gear, necessary toiletries, a shawl or light blanket, a notebook and pen, and a flashlight with extra batteries are useful items to take on a retreat. Check to see if there are any other specific tools you will need, such as a drum or percussion instrument, or a tape recorder. Bear in mind that spiritual centers are not resorts and may be located far from shops.

+ *What not to take:* Most retreat centers ban pets, alcoholic beverages, and all drugs except those prescribed by a doctor. Expect to be asked to leave if you break these rules. Many centers also ask you not to wear perfume or scented toiletries while on retreat, as they can be distracting.

+ *Special needs:* If you have special dietary needs, be sure to discuss them with the retreat center in advance. You may need to bring some of your own food. Also inform the retreat center if you are in a wheelchair or on crutches, or need to sit in a chair for meditation.

to your liking. Many meditation centers, for example, request that no perfume be worn in the meditation room, as it is distracting to other meditators. One woman discovered on her first retreat how closely her identity was tied up with the scent she wore when she felt her fury at being asked to leave the meditation room and take a shower.

Seemingly small considerations can loom large in the confines of a meditation retreat and bring up inner rebellion. Some centers discourage calls to or from the outside world—a challenge to anyone wedded to a cell phone. But often, within hours, you will experience a great sigh of relief at the blessed silence—and at being freed of the competitive demands of daily life that most of us take for granted.

Learning Communities

Another communal environment that offers *sangha* is that of the holistic learning center, such as Omega Institute, located on eighty-two wooded acres near Rhinebeck, New York. (Other well-known learning centers include Esalen Institute in Big Sur, on the California coast—famous as the spawning ground for the human potential movement back in the 1960s—and Hollyhock, on rustic Cortes Island in British Columbia.) A retreat at a learning community, although serious in its focus, may be more relaxed than one at a formal spiritual center. "Summer camp for grown-ups" is how the experience is often fondly described. This is an ideal setting for a first retreat. After a day of stillness you generally have the option to join other people for the evening activities.

Many people return to these centers again and again for a variety of courses and workshops, as their interests broaden and their spiritual commitment deepens. Such communities represent the education of the future: they cater to our desire to build lives with authenticity and meaning. They also hark back to a very ancient tradition—the sacred mystery schools that through shared meditation and movement, song and study, brought the group home to the divine, to God. "Without ritual humans live in solitude," the African medicine man and teacher Malidoma Somé has said.

Group ritual isn't something we have to reserve for special days or formal retreats, however. It can be part of everyday life—as simple as creating a special celebration for a milestone birthday, or blessing a friend's new baby or a new business venture.

For Sylvia Boorstein the test of any spiritual discipline is how well it thrives in the everyday world of work, relationships, and family. "People often tell me they can't get away to meditate," she says. "But that's a myth. Mindful presence and compassion are not things you have to get away to do. They're life."

✍ RESOURCES ✍

BOOKS

Bridges, Holly. *A Circle of Prayer: Coming Together to Find Spirit, Caring, and Community.* Wildcat Canyon Press, 1997.

Caplan, Mariana, ed. *Halfway Up the Mountain.* Prescott, Ariz.: Hohm Press, 1999.

Cooper, David A. *Silence, Simplicity, and Solitude.* Woodstock, Vt.: SkyLight Paths, 1999.

Das, Lama Surya. *Awakening the Buddha Within.* New York: Broadway, 1998.

———. *Awakening to the Sacred.* New York: Broadway, 1999.

McDonnell, Thomas P., ed. *A Thomas Merton Reader.* New York: Doubleday, 1996.

Nhat Hanh, Thich. *Teachings on Love.* Berkeley: Parallax, 1998.

Nhat Hanh, Thich, and friends. *A Joyful Path: Community, Transformation, and Peace.* Berkeley: Parallax, 1994.

Norris, Kathleen. *Amazing Grace.* New York: Riverhead, 1998.

———. *Cloister Walk.* New York: Riverhead, 1996.

———. *Dakota: A Spiritual Geography.* New York: Houghton Mifflin, 1993.

AUDIO/VIDEO

Spiritual Practices and Perspectives for Daily Life. Ram Dass. A three-day retreat with stories and meditation practices from a beloved teacher (Sounds True).

PERIODICALS

Body and Soul: The Annual Guide to Holistic Living
Published by *New Age* magazine
42 Pleasant Street
Watertown, MA 02472
(617) 926–0200

RETREAT CENTERS AND LEARNING COMMUNITIES

For more information on retreats, see *A Guide to Monastic Guest Houses*, by Robert J. Regalbuto (Morehouse, 1998); *Sanctuaries: The Complete United States*, by Jack and Marcia Kelly (Bell Tower, 1996); and *Soul Work: A Field Guide for Spiritual Seekers*, by Anne A. Simpkinson and Charles H. Simpkinson (HarperPerennial, 1998).

Alabama

Benedictine Spirituality and Conference Center of Sacred Heart Monastery. 916 Convent Road, Cullman, AL 35055; (206) 734–8302.

Visitation Monastery. 2300 Spring Hill Avenue, Mobile, AL 36607; (334) 473–2321.

Arizona

Arcosanti. HC-74, Box 4136, Mayer, AZ 86333; (520) 632–7135.

Desert House of Prayer. Box 574, Cortaro, AZ 85652; (520) 744–3825.

The Healing Center of Arizona. 25 Wilson Canyon Road, Sedona, AZ 86336; (520) 282–7710.

California

Abbey of New Clairvaux. 26240 Seventh Street, Vina, CA 96092; (530) 839–2434.

Berkeley Dharmadhatu and Shambhala Center. 2288 Fulton Street, Berkeley, CA 94704; (510) 841–3242.

Dhamma Dena. HC-1, Box 250, Joshua Tree, CA 92252; (760) 362–4815.

Esalen Institute. Highway 1, Big Sur, CA 93920; (408) 667–3000.

Golden Sufi Center. PO Box 428, Inverness, CA 94937; (415) 663–8773.

Green Gulch Farm Zen Center. 1601 Shoreline Highway, Muir Beach, CA 94965; (415) 383–3134.

Harbin Hot Springs Retreat Center. PO Box 782, Middletown, CA 95461; (707) 987–2477.

Mahakankala Buddhist Center. PO Box 4653, Santa Barbara, CA 93140; (805) 965–1813.

Monastery of Mt. Tabor. PO Box 217, 17001 Tomki Road, Redwood Valley, CA 95470; (707) 485–8959.

Mount Cavalry Monastery and Retreat House. PO Box 1296, Santa Barbara, CA 93102; (805) 962–9855.

Mount Madonna Center. 445 Summit Road, Watsonville, CA 95076; (408) 847–0406.

New Camaldoli Hermitage. Big Sur, CA 93920; (408) 667–2456.

Nyingma Institute. 1815 Highland Place, Berkeley, CA 94709; (510) 843–6812.

San Francisco Buddhist Center. 37 Bartlett Street, San Francisco, CA 94110; (415) 282–2018.

San Francisco Zen Center. 300 Page Street, San Francisco, CA 94102; (415) 863–3136.

Shasta Abbey. 3724 Summit Drive, Mt. Shasta, CA 96067; (530) 926–4208.

Sonoma Mountain Zen Center. 6367 Sonoma Mountain Road, Santa Rosa, CA 95404; (707) 545–8105.

Tassajara Zen Mountain Center. 39171 Tassajara Road, Carmel Valley, CA 93924, (415) 431–3771; mailing address: Tassajara Reservations, SF Zen Center, 300 Page Street, San Francisco, CA 94102.

Vedanta Retreat. PO Box 215, Olema, CA 94950; (415) 922–2323.

Zen Hospice Project. 273 Page Street, San Francisco, CA 94102; (415) 863–2910.

Zen Mountain Center. PO Box 43, Mountain Center, CA 92561; (909) 659–5272.

Colorado

Boulder Shambhala Meditation Center. 1345 Spruce Street, Boulder, CO 80302; (303) 444–0190.

Heart of Stillness Retreats. PO Box 106, Jamestown, CO 80455; (303) 459–3431.

St. Benedict's Monastery. 1012 Monastery Road, Snowmass, CO 81654; (970) 927–1162.

Tara Mandala. PO Box 3040, Pagosa Springs, CO 81147; (970) 264–6177.

Florida

Holy Name Monastery. PO Box 2450, 33201 State Road 52, St. Leo, FL 33574; (352) 588–8320.

Georgia

Abbey of Our Lady of the Holy Spirit. 2625 Highway 212 SW, Conyers, GA 30208; (770) 760–0959.

The Loseling Institute. 2531 Briarcliff Road, Suite 101, Atlanta, GA 30329; (404) 982–0051.

Hawaii

Orgyen Dechen Chodzong. PO Box 350, Na'alehu, HI 96772; (808) 929–9505.

St. Isaac's Hermitage. PO Box 731, Mountain View, HI 96771.

Illinois

Udumbara Sangha Zen Center. 501 Sherman, Evanston, IL 60202; (847) 475–3264.

Iowa

New Melleray Abbey. 6500 Melleray Circle, Peosta, IA 52068; (319) 588–2319.

Kentucky

Abbey of Gethsemani. Trappist, KY 40051; (502) 549–3117.

Louisiana

New Orleans Zen Temple. 748 Camp Street, New Orleans, LA 70130; (504) 523–1213.

Maine

Marie Joseph Spiritual Center. RFD 2, Biddeford, ME 04005; (207) 284–5671.

Maryland

Baltimore Shambhala Meditation Center. 11 East Mt. Royal Avenue, Baltimore, MD 21202; (410) 727–2422.

Shambhala Meditation Center of Washington, DC. 8719 Colesville Road, Suite 210, Silver Spring, MD 20910; (301) 588–7020.

Massachusetts

Cambridge Zen Center. 199 Auburn Street, Cambridge, MA 02139; (617) 576–3229.

Eastern Point Retreat House. Gonzaga, Gloucester, MA 10930; (978) 283–0013.

Emery House. The Society of St. John the Evangelist, Emery Lane, West Newbury, MA 01985; (978) 462–7940.

Glastonbury Abbey. The Retreat House, 16 Hull Street, Hingham, MA 02043; (781) 749–2155.

Insight Meditation Society. 1230 Pleasant Street, Barre, MA 01005; (978) 355–4378.

Kripalu Center for Yoga and Health. PO Box 793, Lenox, MA 01240; (413) 448–3400.

Rowe Camp and Conference Center. Kings Highway Road, Rowe, MA 01367; (413) 339–4954.

Michigan

Deep Spring Center. 3455 Charing Cross Road, Ann Arbor, MI 48108; (734) 971–3455.

St. Augustine's House. PO Box 125, Oxford, MI 48371; (248) 628–5155.

Zen Buddhist Temple. 48104 Packard Road, Ann Arbor, MI 48104; (734) 761–6520.

Minnesota

Minneapolis Shambhala Meditation Center. 1304 University Avenue NE, Minneapolis, MN 55413; (612) 331–7737.

Missouri

Maria Fonte Solitude. 6150 Antire Road, High Ridge, MO 63049; (314) 677–3235.

Montana

Feathered Pipe Ranch. PO Box 1682, Helena, MT 59624; (406) 442–8196.

New Jersey

Carmel Retreat. 1071 Ramapo Valley Road, Mahwah, NJ 07430; (201) 327–7090.

St. Marguerite's Retreat House. Convent of St. John Baptist, PO Box 240, Mendham, NJ 07945; (973) 543–4641.

New Mexico

Center for Action and Contemplation. PO Box 12464, Albuquerque, NM 87195; (505) 242–9588.

Lama Foundation. PO Box 240, San Cristobal, NM 87564; (505) 586–1269.

Pecos Benedictine Monastery. PO Box 1080, Pecos, NM 87552; (505) 757–6415.

Upaya Foundation. 1404 Cerro Gordo Road, Santa Fe, NM 87501; (505) 986–8518.

New York

Abode of the Message. 5 Abode Road, New Lebanon, NY 12125; (518) 794–8090.

Amitabha Foundation. PO Box 25577, Rochester, NY 14625; (716) 442–5853.

Cormaria Center. PO Box 1993, Sag Harbor, NY 11963; (516) 725–4206.

Dai Bosatsu Zendo. HCR 1, Box 171, Livingston Manor, NY 12758; (914) 439–4566.

Elat Chayyim. 99 Mill Hook Road, Accord, NY 12404; (800) 398–2630.

Holy Cross Monastery. Box 99, Route 9W, West Park, NY 12493; (914) 384–6660.

New York Shambhala Center. 118 West Twenty-second Street, New York, NY 10011; (212) 675–6544.

New York Open Center. 83 Spring Street, New York, NY 10012; (212) 219–2527.

New York Zendo Shobo-ji. 223 East Sixty-seventh Street, New York, NY 10021; (212) 861–3333.

Omega Institute for Holistic Studies. 260 Lake Drive, Rhinebeck, NY 12572; (914) 266–4444.

Springwater Center. 7179 Mill Street, Springwater, NY 14560; (716) 669–2141.

Still Point House of Prayer. Route 423, Box 53, Stillwater, NY 12170; (518) 587–4967.

Wellsprings. 93 Maple Street, Glen Falls, NY 12801; (518) 792–3183.

Zen Center of New York City. 119 West Twenty-third Street, Room 907, New York, NY 10011; (212) 642–1591.

Zen Mountain Monastery. Box 197, South Plank Road, Mt. Tremper, NY 12457; (914) 688–2228.

North Carolina

Avila Retreat Center. 711 Mason Road, Durham, NC 27712; (919) 477–1285.

Southern Dharma Retreat Center. 1661 West Road, Hot Springs, NC 28743; (828) 622–7112.

North Dakota

Annunciation Priory. 7250 University Drive, Bismarck, ND 58504; (701) 255–1520.

Ohio

Jesuit Retreat House. 5629 State Road, Cleveland, OH 44134; (440) 884–9300.

Oregon

Breitenbush Hot Springs. PO Box 578, Detroit, OR 97342; (503) 854–3314.

Mt. Angel Abbey Retreat House. St. Benedict, OR 97373; (503) 845–3025.

Shalom Prayer Center. 840 South Main Street, Mt. Angel, OR 97362; (503) 845–6773.

Pennsylvania

Daylesford Abbey. 220 South Valley Road, Paoli, PA 19301; (610) 647–2530.

Kirkridge. RR3, Box 3402, Bangor, PA 18013; (215) 588–1793.

Pendle Hill. 338 Plush Mill Road, Wallingford, PA 19086; (800) 742–3150.

Philadelphia Shambhala Meditation Center. 2030 Sansom Street, Philadelphia, PA 19103; (215) 568–6070.

St. Raphaela Mary Retreat House. 616 Coopertown Road, Haverford, PA 19041; (610) 642–5715.

South Carolina

Springbank Retreat Center. Rt. 2, Box 180, Kingstree, SC 29556; (800) 671–0361.

Tennessee

Penuel Ridge Retreat Center. 1440 Sam's Creek Road, Ashland City, TN 37015; (615) 792–3734.

Texas

Austin Shambhala Meditation Center. 1702 South Fifth Street, Austin, TX 78704; (512) 443–3263.

Corpus Christi Abbey. HCR 2, Box 6300, Sandia, TX 78383; (512) 547–3257.

Utah

Abbey of Our Lady of the Holy Trinity. 1250 South 9500 East, Huntsville, UT 84317; (801) 745–3784.

Vermont

Karmê-Chöling. 369 Patneaude Lane, Barnet, VT 05821; (802) 633–2384.

Virginia

Holy Cross Abbey. Route 2, Box 3870, Berryville, VA 22611; (540) 955–3124.

Satchidananda Ashram-Yogaville. Route 1, Box 120, Buckingham, VA 23921; (804) 969–3121.

Washington

Chinook Learning Center. PO Box 57, Clinton, WA 98236; (360) 221–3153.

Cloud Mountain Retreat Center. 373 Agren Road, Castle Rock, WA 98611; (360) 274–4859.

Kairos House of Prayer. West 1714 Stearns Road, Spokane, WA 99208; (509) 466–2187.

Shambhala Center of Seattle. 919 East Pike Street, Third Floor, Seattle, WA 98122; (206) 860–4060.

West Virginia

Bhavana Society. Route 1, Box 218–3, High View, WV 26808; (304) 856–3241.

Wisconsin
Siena Center. 5635 Erie Street, Racine, WI 53402; (414) 639–4100.

Canada
Hollyhock. Box 127, Manson's Landing, Cortes Island, BC V0P 1K0; (800) 933–6339.

12.

Into Action

My life is my message.
—MAHATMA GANDHI

By now you have undoubtedly begun a spiritual practice and perhaps even found a community to practice with. Once you have settled into your practice, you will begin to discover the joy of contemplative living—the moment-to-moment feeling of being fully alive, of being centered and present regardless of what is happening around you. Inner peace, in short.

Every so often, you may want to try an experiment: Skip your formal prayer or meditation for a few days. The purpose is not to take a vacation from contemplation but to experience the sacred in everyday life. "The true saint," the Sufis teach, "goes in and out amongst the people and eats and sleeps with them and buys and sells in the market and takes part in social intercourse—and never forgets God for a single moment." This is the last of the ten Zen Ox-Herding pictures we encountered in Chapter I. It is the fruit of the spiritual quest, the essence of the contemplative life.

Bringing a sense of awareness to ordinary activities takes intention, but it doesn't have to take a lot of effort. Teachers like the Vietnamese Zen monk Thich Nhat Hanh show us that mindfulness becomes simply the lens through which we see our day, bringing into sharper focus the grace of God and the divine connection of all beings. The equanimity we discover in prayer and meditation is available to us anytime, if we pay attention.

"When we see a red light or a stop sign," Thich Nhat Hanh writes in *Present Moment, Wonderful Moment*, "we can smile at it and thank it, because it is a *bodhisattva* helping us to return to the present moment. The red light is a bell of mindfulness. We may have thought of it as an enemy, preventing us from achieving our goal. But now we know the red light is our friend, helping us resist rushing and calling us to return to the present moment where we can meet with life, joy, and peace."

Small moments in everyday life can be our teachers. One woman even uses the electronic security system at her office entryway as her "red light," reminding her to slow down and become aware. To open the door, she must place her ID card against a plate on the wall. "I've discovered that you literally have to *caress* the plate with your card," she says. "If you hurry or jab at the plate, the door won't budge. That door is teaching me not only patience but respect for inanimate objects."

Practicing mindfulness in daily life also equips you for those times when your circumstances don't leave time for formal meditation or prayer. In *A Heart as Wide as the World* Sharon Salzberg writes about a conversation between a meditation teacher, Munindra, and his student, Kamala, who insisted that her life as a single mother of two did not permit her to sit in meditation every day.

Finally, perhaps seeing that her protest had reason, he asked her what she did more than anything else each day. She thought for a moment, then responded: "Wash dishes." Munindra went over to the sink with her, and together they practiced mindful dishwashing.

Then Munindra noticed that in the short, dark hallway between Kamala's bedroom and the rest of the house, the children tended to leave her alone. He suggested that she consider the hallway a temple for walking meditation. Whenever Kamala was in that part of the house, she practiced mindfully walking those few steps. . . . Because she was so aware, she came to regard that hallway as a sacred site.

As the practice of ordinary mindfulness or contemplative awareness sharpens your senses, you may notice a difference in the way you experience some of the most rudimentary aspects of life. Your taste in food, for example, may change. Once you are more sensitive to your body and its needs, the chocolate treat you once craved—while still delicious—may seem too rich to finish.

Here's an experiment you can do by yourself or with others. First, prepare a simple meal. Practice mindfulness in the kitchen, moving with intention and care as you wash the vegetables, sort the grains, chop the fruit, stir a sauce into steaming pasta.

Try This: Food for Thought

According to the yogi Swami Sivananda, "Purity of mind depends on the purity of food." Those who find solace in meditation and prayer may become sensitive to the power of food. The Yogic scriptures divide food into three types: *sattvic,* or pure; *rajasic,* or stimulating; and *tamasic,* or impure and static.

Sattvic foods are believed to promote health, vitality, strength, and tranquillity. They include raw fruits and raw or lightly cooked vegetables, nuts, seeds, legumes, whole grain bread, herbal tea, and dairy products such as cheese and butter.

Rajasic foods create a distracting, restless state of mind, or might bring about the jitters. Foods in a Rajasic diet include stimulants such as onion, garlic, coffee, tea, sugary foods (yes, even chocolate), and spicy and salted foods. Tobacco is also considered rajasic.

Tamasic foods are said to increase feelings of laziness and decrease motivation, and are associated with depression. Tamasic items are meat, fish, eggs, drugs, and alcohol, as well as any foods that have been fermented, burned, fried, or reheated many times. Overeating is considered tamasic.

As you practice being mindful in your everyday life, notice whether or not you begin to sense these subtle energies in your food.

Remain attentive even as you busy yourself with the smallest tasks—uncorking the olive oil, tossing the broccoli stalks into the composter.

Take time to present the meal in a pleasing way. Set the table with your prettiest china and linens. Add a bouquet of flowers. Before you begin to eat, offer silent thanks for the meal. There is a lovely verse said before meals at Dai Bosatsu Zendo that expresses appreciation for everyone involved in growing and preparing the food, and acknowledges our place in the community of all beings:

> *First, let us reflect on our own work and the effort of those who brought us this food.*
> *Secondly, let us be aware of the quality of our deeds as we receive this meal.*
> *Thirdly, what is most essential is the practice of mindfulness, which helps us transcend greed, anger, and delusion.*
> *Fourthly, we appreciate this food, which sustains the good health of our body and mind.*
> *Fifthly, in order to continue our practice for all beings we accept this offering.*

Continue the silence throughout the meal. As you eat, focus your attention on the food. Notice the colors, the flavors, the textures, the temperature, of each mouthful.

Eating mindfully, you will be more aware of the moment you become full. You may have the feeling of "enough" sooner than you are used to. Honor that feeling and stop eating, even if you have not finished everything on your plate.

After the meal, reflect on how the experience differed from your usual eating style. This practice is one you can apply to every activity in your everyday life. Think how different mindful ironing would be—or mindful dog-washing or floor-scrubbing or memo-writing.

Another way to practice ordinary mindfulness is to stop periodically and bring yourself back to the present. (Wouldn't it be wonderful to have a kind of inner cruise-control that buzzed whenever your mind wandered?) You can use various trigger behaviors as your reminder. For instance, when you become aware that you're ensnared in a negative reaction or you realize you're rushing too fast, you can stop and focus on your breathing. That will automatically bring you back to the present moment.

Everyone is in a hurry these days. Meeting the number of obligations we face requires a lot of juggling. But an overbooked day does not have to generate overlooked moments. "Rushing does not have to do with speed," Insight meditation teacher

Joseph Goldstein writes in *Transforming the Mind, Healing the World*. "You can rush moving slowly, and you can rush moving quickly."

Rushing in itself can be a spiritual "heads-up," Goldstein suggests. "The feeling of rushing is good feedback. Whenever we are not present, right then, in that situation, we should stop and take a few breaths. Settle into the body again. Feel yourself sitting. Feel the step of a walk. Be in your body."

When your thoughts wander in a business meeting, for example, concentrating on the steady in and out of your breath will return your attention to what's going on in the room. This is what the sixteenth-century French essayist Montaigne called bringing your thoughts "back again to the walk."

> *When I dance, I dance. When I sleep, I sleep; yes, and when I walk alone in a beautiful orchard, if my thoughts have been concerned with extraneous incidents for some part of the time, for some other part I lead them back again to the walk, to the orchard, to the sweetness of this solitude, and to myself.*

Being present is a practice of recognizing the signs of distraction and responding gently to bringing your mind back. "Rest does not come from sleeping," *A Course in Miracles* teaches us, "but from waking."

Awake, we can experience the sacred in every moment.

How Can I Help?

There will almost certainly come a time when you discover that prayer and meditation are no longer their own reward. The contemplative life is, ultimately, a life of action. You may yearn to take the experience of grace or peace or energy that you have cultivated in your practice and use it to heal or serve or promote justice in the world. This desire is a natural extension of spiritual practice. Looking deeply within does not mean seeing the external world with passive eyes. When it comes to taking action, nothing can effect positive change quite like the insights gained from sitting still. In *How Can I Help?* Ram Dass and Paul Gorman—longtime spiritual activists—note the question posed in the book title is a "timeless quest of the heart." In other words, *what am I called to do to ease the pain and suffering in the world around me?*

Both the Chinese and Japanese languages use the same character for *mind* and *heart* (*hsin* in Chinese; *shin* in Japanese). In contemplative life we learn that when the mind is clear, "the heart hungers for that new social order wherein justice dwells," as Dorothy Day wrote in *The Catholic Worker*.

Becoming more present to, and mindful of, all life includes becoming more aware of the pain of others. "Seeing suffering has a way of getting inside you," says Sister Helen Prejean, whose work on integrating faith and justice was chronicled in the book and movie *Dead Man Walking*. "When you see the injustice that's causing the suffering, you've got to do something about it. Otherwise, you become complicit."

The blending of politics or social action and spirituality has a long history. "God is justice," wrote the late-fourteenth-century English mystic Julian of Norwich, and five hundred years later Gandhi said, "Those who say religion has nothing to do with politics do not know what religion means." Many spiritual leaders were active in the civil rights and antiwar movements of the Sixties.

One teacher who clearly demonstrates faith in action is Bernard Glassman Roshi, cofounder of the Zen Peacemaker Order. Over the years he and his students and associates have founded and run many community-based businesses in the South Bronx area of New York. Glassman is also known for his "street retreats"—silent meditations that involve such unlikely activities as living on the sidewalks of Manhattan's infamous Bowery to find out how it feels to be homeless. For several years Glassman has taken groups to meditate in the former death camp at Auschwitz. Such activities are powerful ways to hone compassion and awareness.

"It is a myth," Glassman writes in *Bearing Witness: A Zen Master's Lessons in Making Peace*, "that spiritual people are not attached, that they're somehow above the trials and tribulations of ordinary life. They're tremendously affected by them. For rather than living in the realm of ideas . . . they live in the realm of action."

In most mystical traditions, Glassman explains, the mystic's role is that of the healer, the peacemaker, the one who makes things whole. If you want to be of service but don't know what to do, "bearing witness is a good place to start," he suggests. When you do that, he says, "The right action arises by itself. We don't have to worry about what to do. We don't have to figure out solutions ahead of time. Once we listen with our entire body and mind, loving action arises."

Right Action

Loving action is Right Action—the fourth principle of the Buddha's Eightfold path to enlightenment. The teaching of Right Action is karma: what we sow, shall we reap. If our actions plant seeds of peace, we will live in peace, even if the world around us is at war. But if our actions grow from bitterness or hate, our lives will be sorrowful, no matter what kind of paradise our surroundings offer.

Part of *bearing witness* is being alert in every moment so that you can understand what the "next right action" should be. It can be as simple as remaining patient and courteous in a crowded checkout line, or listening empathetically to a friend. Right action can also mean volunteering in a hospice or school or for an international relief organization, or working for a political or environmental cause.

In a conscious life every gesture counts. Sulak Sivaraksa, nominated twice for the Nobel Peace Prize, writes in *Seeds of Peace*, "Buddhism with a small *b* [exists] where Buddhism enters the life of a society through the presence of men and women who practice and demonstrate the Way . . . through their thoughts, speech, and actions."

In *The Ecstatic Journey*, author Sophie Burnham writes of the "hidden mystics"— people who "never even think about God" but nonetheless go about their business quietly living in the presence of the sacred. Some are doing good works in the world; others merely radiate a quality of being we recognize as holy. The newspaper seller, your child's teacher, the woman next to you on the bus—any one of them could be walking the path of the everyday mystic.

Transmuting Suffering

As we can see, sooner or later being mindful in our actions brings us face to face with the enormous suffering of others. And the heart that bears witness longs to serve. The Tibetan Buddhist teacher Chögyam Trungpa called it the "genuine heart of sadness" of the spiritual warrior. In *Shambhala: The Sacred Path of the Warrior*, he explains:

> When you awaken your heart in this way you find, to your surprise, that your heart is empty. . . . If you search for awakened heart, if you put your hand through your rib cage and feel for it, there is nothing there except for tenderness. You feel sore and soft . . . because your heart is completely exposed. . . . The genuine heart of sadness comes from feeling that your nonexistent heart is full. . . . For the warrior this experience of sad and tender heart is what gives birth to fearlessness.

The bridge that links fearlessness to action is compassion. "Compassion is the strength that arises out of seeing the true nature of suffering in the world," Sharon Salzberg explains in *Lovingkindness*. "Compassion allows us to bear witness to that suffering, whether it is in ourselves or others, without fear; it allows us to name injustice without hesitation, and to act strongly, with all the skill at our disposal."

Compassion connects the pain we see in others back to our own pain. As the Trappist monk Thomas Merton explained in the essay "A Body of Broken Bones," "I cannot treat other men unless I have compassion for them. I must at least have enough compassion to realize that when they suffer they feel somewhat as I do when I suffer. And if for some reason I do not spontaneously feel this kind of sympathy for others, then it is God's will that I do what I can to learn how."

Compassion in Action

Compassion is not just an attitude of caring and kindness, or even empathy. It is also a political stance. Thich Nhat Hanh told writer Trevor Carolan that he developed what is now called Engaged Buddhism "so we could continue our contemplative life in the midst of helping the victims of war. We worked to relieve the suffering while trying to maintain our own mindfulness."

Few understand this practice as well as Aung San Suu Kyi, awarded the Nobel Peace Prize in 1991 for her nonviolent struggle for democracy and human rights in her native Burma. "Engaged Buddhism is active compassion or active *metta*," she explained in an interview for *Shambhala Sun*. "It means doing something about the situation by bringing whatever relief you can to those who need it most, by caring for them, by doing what you can to help others."

You cannot reach others with compassion, however, unless you have touched the pain in your own heart. In Chapter 6 we explored some of the practices, such as *metta* (lovingkindness) and *tonglen* (giving and receiving), that can open us to self-forgiveness and, from there, to forgiveness for others. "The ground for compassion is established first by practicing sensitivity toward ourselves," the *Vipassana* teacher Jack Kornfield writes in *A Path with Heart*. "Compassion for others gives rise to the power to transform resentment into forgiveness, hatred into friendliness, and fear into respect for all beings. True compassion arises from a sense that the heart has the fearless capacity to embrace all things, to touch all things, to relate to all things."

The way we speak, the gestures we use, the choices we make in every interaction— all these have an impact on others. When we act consciously and intentionally, we send a signal that it is possible to live with a peaceful heart. That in itself is a great service in today's world.

The Web of Life

For many people increased awareness in everyday life brings a feeling of connection to the earth and all beings. As you cultivate true compassion you may experience this interconnectedness as concern for the environment, a sense of stewardship for the earth and all its creatures. "Sangha does not stop at the threshold of our species and next of kin," Joan Halifax Roshi of the Zen Peacemaker Order states in an essay included in the anthology *Dharma Gaia.* As Mobi Ho, a translator of Thich Nhat Hanh's work, puts it, "Mindfulness nurtures our ability to see deeply into our true nature. The view of a humanity that stands isolated or above other forms of life dissolves."

This is the message that Chief Seattle of the Suquamish Indians passed down to us in 1854: "Man did not weave the web of life, he is merely a strand in it. Whatever he does to the web, he does to himself."

The interdependence of life is the theme of Indra's Net, an ancient Chinese legend likening the universe to a net woven of pearls, each of which reflects the others, suggesting the interconnectedness of all. Contemplative living makes us aware that each of us is a divinely inspired individual and at the same time, a jewel in Indra's net.

Somewhere along the spiritual path we may experience a moment of feeling at one with the divine. In that second the web of life becomes apparent in all its glory. Day to day we practice our meditation and prayer, try to live consciously and with concern for one another. The joy of contemplative life, as the poet William Blake wrote, is that at last we see "a world in a grain of sand, and a heaven in a wild flower." What we sought was here inside us, all along.

RESOURCES

BOOKS

A Course in Miracles. New York: Viking, 1996.

Badiner, Allan Hunt, ed. *Dharma Gaia.* Berkeley: Parallax, 1990.

Burnham, Sophie. *The Ecstatic Journey.* New York: Ballantine, 1997.

Das, Lama Surya. *Awakening to the Sacred.* New York: Broadway, 1999.

Dass, Ram, and Paul Gorman. *How Can I Help?* New York: Alfred A. Knopf, 1997.

Eppsteiner, Fred, ed. *The Path of Compassion: Writings on Socially Engaged Buddhism.* Berkeley: Parallax, 1988.

Fox, Matthew. *Original Blessing.* Santa Fe: Bear and Company, 1986.

Glassman, Bernard, Roshi. *Bearing Witness: A Zen Master's Lessons in Making Peace.* New York: Bell Tower, 1998.

Goldstein, Joseph. *Transforming the Mind, Healing the World*. Mahwah, NJ: Paulist Press, 1994.

Kornfield, Jack. *A Path with Heart*. New York: Bantam, 1993.

Kotler, Arnold, ed. *Engaged Buddhist Reader*. Berkeley: Parallax, 1996.

McDonnell, Thomas P. *A Thomas Merton Reader*. New York: Doubleday, 1996.

Mitchell, Stephen, ed. *The Enlightened Mind: An Anthology of Sacred Prose*. New York: HarperCollins, 1991.

————. *The Essence of Wisdom: Words from Masters to Illuminate the Spiritual Path*. New York: Broadway, 1998.

Nhat Hanh, Thich. *Present Moment, Wonderful Moment*. Berkeley: Parallax, 1990.

Salzberg, Sharon. *A Heart as Wide as the World*. Boston: Shambhala, 1997.

Sivaraksa, Sulak. *Seeds of Peace*. Berkeley: Parallax, 1991.

Smith, Jean, ed. *Everyday Mind: 366 Reflections on the Buddhist Path*. New York: Riverhead, 1997.

Trungpa, Chögyam. *Shambhala: The Sacred Path of the Warrior*. Boston: Shambhala, 1988.

AUDIO/VIDEO

Road Sage. Sylvia Boorstein. Mindfulness techniques for dealing with the stresses of driving (Sounds True).

Sacred Practices for Conscious Living. Nancy Napier. Guided meditation exercises to support mindful living and experiencing the sacred in daily life (Nancy J. Napier).

Permissions

Dr. Lauren Artress, excerpts from *Walking a Sacred Path: Rediscovering the Labyrinth as a Spiritual Tool.* Copyright © 1995 by Lauren Artress. Reprinted with the permission of Putnam Berkeley, a division of Penguin Putnam Inc.

Perle Besserman, excerpt adapted from *The Shambhala Guide to Kabbalah and Jewish Mysticism.* Copyright © 1997 by Perle Besserman. Reprinted with the permission of Shambhala Publications, Inc.

Joan Borysenko, excerpts from *The Ways of the Mystic: Seven Paths to God.* Copyright © 1997 by Joan Borysenko. Reprinted with the permission of Hay House.

Byron Brown, excerpt from *Soul without Shame: A Guide to Liberating Yourself from the Judge Within.* Copyright © 1999 by Byron Brown. Reprinted with the permission of Shambhala Publications, Inc.

Don G. Campbell, excerpts from *The Roar of Silence: Healing Powers of Breath, Tone & Music.* Copyright © 1989 by Don G. Campbell. Reprinted with the permission of The Theosophical Publishing House.

Peter Chin Kean Choy, excerpts from *T'ai Chi, Chi Kung: Fifteen Ways to a Happier You.* Copyright © 1999 by Peter Chin Kean Choy. Reprinted with the permission of The Overlook Press.

Lama Surya Das, excerpts from *Awakening the Buddha Within: Eight Steps to Enlightenment.* Copyright © 1997 by Lama Surya Das. Reprinted with the permission of Broadway Books, a division of Random House, Inc.

Index